DATE		

GARDENING WITH BIBLICAL PLANTS

HANDBOOK FOR THE HOME GARDENER

GARDENING WITH BIBLICAL PLANTS

HANDBOOK FOR THE HOME GARDENER

Wilma James
Illustrated by Arla Lippsmeyer

NELSON-HALL 𝑛𝒉 CHICAGO

LIBRARY OF CONGRESS CATALOGING IN PUBLICATION DATA

James, Wilma Roberts, 1905–
  Gardening with biblical plants.

  Bibliography: p.
  Includes index.
  1. Plants in the Bible. 2. Gardening. I. Title.
SB454.3.B52J35   1983   635.9'51'56194   83–2290
ISBN 0–8304–1009–0

Manufactured in the United States of America

10 9 8 7 6 5 4 3 2 1

The paper in this book is pH neutral (acid-free).

CONTENTS

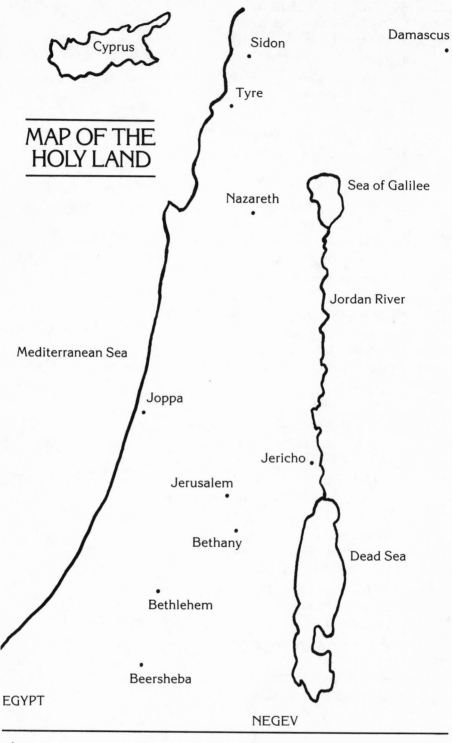

MAP OF THE
HOLY LAND

Cyprus

Sidon

Damascus

Tyre

Nazareth

Sea of Galilee

Jordan River

Mediterranean Sea

Joppa

Jericho

Jerusalem

Bethany

Dead Sea

Bethlehem

Beersheba

EGYPT

NEGEV

INTRODUCTION

G ardening with Bible lands plants is bound to reap rich rewards. Whether you garden indoors or out, you experience a sense of God's presence while working with plants that kept company with Bible-time people and become more aware of the important role plants played in the stories of the Scriptures. In addition, by associating each plant with the special message set forth in God's Word, a never-ending source of spiritual enrichment is received.

Recorded throughout the Bible are hundreds of verses pertaining to plants. Many of the plant names are well known today and can be accepted readily as the plants' correct names. Establishing definite identification of others is frequently a difficult and lengthy task. In some instances plants that once grew in the Holy Land and Egypt no longer exist or may be referred to in general terms such as "vines," "grasses," and "spices." Centuries of translation and interpretation have obscured the identities of some plants that were familiar to the authors of the Bible. Due to extensive research by professional botanists and theological scholars, an accordance has been reached on the names of numerous plants which were formerly in doubt. Plants still causing much disagreement among Bible translators are omitted from this book.

Plant names are taken primarily from the King James (Authorized) Version. A few have been drawn from other versions and their sources are duly noted in the text. In many cases, only the portion of the verse relevant to the plant cited is quoted. Verse numbers are also given to assist the reader.

The two-word Latin labels (scientific names) follow the common or popular name of each plant, the genus name (written with a capital letter) precedes the name of the species. Thus, the Latin label for the fig is *Ficus carica.* Since Latin names remain the same on any plant list and common names vary from one region to another, it is necessary to know the Latin name in order to correctly identify each plant.

The vast majority of biblical plants named in this book thrive somewhere in the United States. The plants or seeds can be obtained from local nurseries or ordered through garden supply catalogs. Close-at-hand kinds may be propagated from cuttings. In cases where named species are not at all available, similar plants of the same genus can be substituted. They will be near enough in appearance to represent the plant mentioned in the Bible passage.

People who are especially interested in growing Bible-land plants are often town or city dwellers with window gardens or small yards. Even with limited space it is possible to prepare a bowl garden based on biblical plants. What material you use depends upon the setting you wish to create. For example, you could make a miniature biblical scene by including "the fir tree, the pine tree, and the box" (Isaiah 60:13). Eventually plants used in a miniature garden outgrow their container. When they reach that stage, they can be replanted in individual pots or in the open ground.

A sunny outdoor space might present a biblical food plant scene, exhibiting the "cucumbers, and the melons, and the leeks, and the onions, and the garlic" the Israelites longed for in Numbers 11:5. A tub partially filled with sand and sunk in the ground could display water plants like the "bulrushes" and the "flags" (Exodus 2:3), the "reeds" and "papyrus" (Isaiah 19:6-7), with fragrant mint edging the tub (Luke 11:42). Other groupings might consist of flowers, fruit trees, or herbs named in the Bible. Groupings of brook, desert, oasis, and meadow plants could emphasize the diversity of climates found in the Holy Land. The possibilities for themes are virtually endless.

This book is meant to be a guide, one presenting a listing of over one hundred biblical plants and their messages of the Scriptures. It tells how to grow individual plants indoors and outdoors and suggests ways to adapt them to various situations. Each plant is illustrated by a line drawing to help with identification. There follows a glossary, a bibliography, and an index. Along the way the gardener will want to turn again to the Bible to discover the extent of the marvelous plants the Creator fashioned to fulfill the needs of His people.

GARDENING WITH BIBLICAL PLANTS

HANDBOOK FOR THE HOME GARDENER

PART 1

Shrubs and Trees

And out of the ground made the Lord God to grow every tree that is pleasant to sight, and good for food.
(Genesis 2:9)

In describing the Garden of Eden, the author of Genesis tells of the trees God so bountifully provided for human pleasure and use. Cited in the Bible are a large number of shrubs and trees, all of which were, and still are, appreciated for their food, oil, resins, lumber, shade, or beauty. Trees were held so sacred by ancient Hebrews as gifts of God that their annual first-ripe fruits were dedicated to Him (Exodus 22:22). Deuteronomy instructs not to destroy fruit-bearing trees when attacking cities "for the tree of the field is man's life" (20:19). Orchards and other choice plants were protected from wild animals and thieves by walls or thorny hedges.

Specific trees of the forest, woodlands, and deserts were venerated, and there are countless allusions to trees by Hebrew prophets and biblical writers who used them to reinforce the Word of God. Valuable timber trees such as cedar, pine, and spruce were sought for the construction of buildings, chests, images, musical instruments, and coffins. Through greed and carelessness, mankind caused barrenness and desolation in many areas of the Holy Land where trees once flourished. For example, the cedars of Lebanon are now almost extinct, decimated by years of cutting without replenishment. King Solomon alone sent more than 180,000 men to Lebanon to procure cedar trunks to be incorporated into his temple (I Kings 5:13–18).

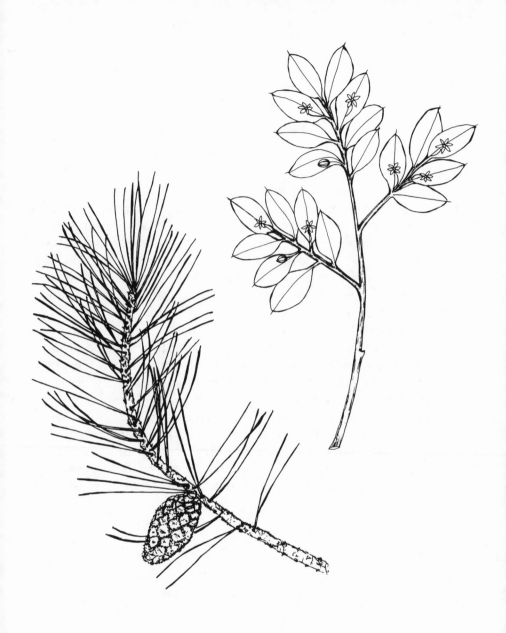

But the living, growing plants of God's world do not necessarily have to be big for us to enjoy. Seedlings planted in a low bowl give the impression of natural-sized trees in miniature. The size of the bowl may vary, yet it should be at least four inches deep to allow the plant roots plenty of space in which to grow. A thick layer of coarse gravel placed in the bottom of the bowl is essential for drainage. For soil, a mixture of equal parts of loam, peat moss, and sand may be used, or a commercially packaged potting mixture will do. The plants are arranged in a predetermined design, the soil tamped into place and watered just enough to settle the roots. Thereafter the soil must be kept evenly moist but not wet. In winter, bowl gardens require a site by a sunny window and benefit during the summer months if set outside under the shade of a large tree or on a patio.

Biblical shrubs and trees that are unable to withstand freezing temperatures should be grown in pots or tubs and moved indoors for winter protection. Small or medium-sized plants may be placed by a window or in a cool room where there is lots of light. An unheated but not extremely cold basement or garage will provide storage for plants grown in larger tubs, for example, the tender trees such as carob, date palm, and olive.

A great amount of pleasure may be gained in watching a plant develop from a seedling, but be aware that the seeds of many shrubs and trees germinate slowly. Hard-shelled seeds such as the acacia, apricot, and almond germinate faster if they are soaked in warm water for two or three days. Poke the softened wet seeds into soil-filled pots, placing two or three seeds in each hole.

In sowing small seeds, spread gravel in the bottom of a wooden flat or a shallow pot, and add a 2-inch layer of soil. Furrows should be about one-fourth inch deep and the seeds arranged about 3 inches apart. The soil is then pressed over them, watered with a fine spray, and the container placed where it will receive morning sun. While waiting for the seeds to sprout, adequate moist conditions are of utmost importance. Not all the seeds will germinate, but those that do should be thinned to the strongest seedlings.

Generally, when the seedlings are one year old, they can be repotted. Cut them out of their container carefully with a knife. They may be planted singly in pots or in the open soil where they will grow faster. After another year of growth, the seedlings can be taken up and transferred to permanent locations.

ACACIA

Acacia seyal, A. tortilis
Biblical term: Shittim wood

WHILE THE HEBREWS WERE sojourning in the wilderness, God revealed to the prophet Moses a specific plan for building the sacred Ark of the Covenant. The acacia-wood Ark was to contain the two stone tablets on which were recorded the covenant between God and Israel and to support a gold-covered mercy seat upon which God would be invisibly enthroned as He communicated with His people (Exodus 25:10–22). Of primary importance were the acacia-wood carrying poles attached to the Ark, for they assured its portability. Thus the presence of God would be ever with the Israelites while they traveled in the desert.

Bible references to the acacia are almost entirely reserved to the Israelites' wanderings in the Sinai peninsula, to the use of its wood in building the Ark, and to the fittings of the Tabernacle (Exodus 25, 26, 27:1). These thorny trees are still common in the Sinai area, growing in wadies where water sweeps down during the rainy season.

The acacia tree reaches a height of 20 to 25 feet even in waste places, but is frequently shrubby in appearance. It has soft, feathery foliage and in early spring is covered with sprays of fragrant yellow blossoms which produce fruit capsules resembling a pea pod. The rough orange-brown bark encases a hard, fine-grained, and insect-resistant wood. Along with these qualities and its presence on the desert, the acacia was ideal for a building material.

The fast-growing, free-flowering acacia is easily cultivated outdoors in subtropical zones and elsewhere in pots or tubs to be wintered indoors. Keep the plant well-watered at first. Once established it becomes drought resistant and requires little water.

To create a miniature replica of the desert in nature, the terrain in a bowl garden should be basically flat, with a topping of sand and a few rocky ledges. A large rock could suggest the mountain upon which the Law was given to Moses. Use gravel or pebbles to simulate a wadi, and on each side of the wadi insert acacia seedlings. Small, appropriate figurines would add interest to the scene.

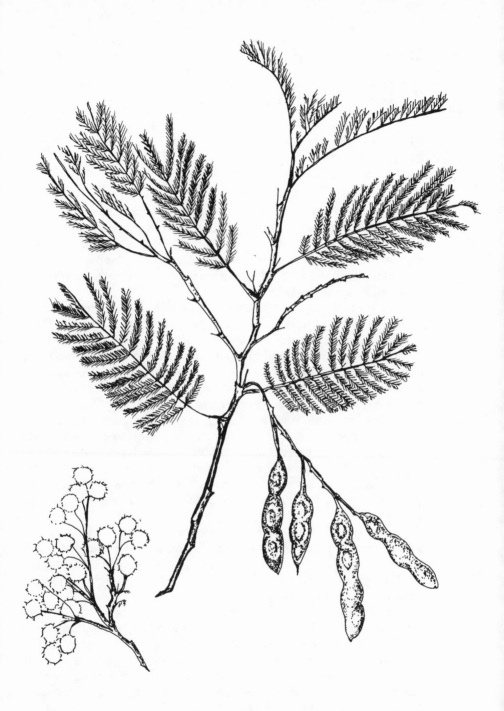

And they shall make an ark of shittim wood.
Exodus 25:10

ALEPPO PINE, JERUSALEM PINE

Pinus halepensis
Biblical term: Fir

THE MOST SIGNIFICANT STRUCTURE built under King Solomon's sponsorship was the magnificent Jerusalem Temple. Through formal agreements with his ally, King Hiram of Tyre, Solomon obtained architects, workmen, and building materials to construct the splendid edifice (I Kings 6:11–14).

Timbers of this most desirable pine were imported along with the cedars from the forests of Hiram to be used in the flooring (I Kings 6:15), in doors (6:34), and in ceilings (II Chronicles 3:5) of the temple. Ezekiel states that this building material was transported from Senir (27:5), the Amorite name for majestic Mount Hermon. Aleppo pines now grow abundantly on the dry, rocky hillsides of ancient Palestine, eventually reaching a height of 60 feet.

Often nearly columnar in shape, the evergreen and highly ornamental Aleppo pine produces long, slender, light-green needles and bears oval, reddish to yellow-brown cones which take two or three years to ripen. The tree thrives in desert heat, drought, and wind, and rocky, sandy, or poor soils, but grows best in full sun. Although tender when young, an established tree can withstand near-zero temperatures.

An Aleppo pine will add a woodsy atmosphere to any garden, being most useful in areas where poor soils and arid climates prevail. A small tree can be grown in a box to restrict its size, yet will display the exact features of a towering forest tree. Plenty of sunlight and a well-drained soil are obligatory in either instance.

A miniature forest of Aleppo pine and cedars of Lebanon seedlings, planted in a bowl together, would be in keeping with the Bible passage. The soil can be mounded up to represent a tiny mountain and some small stones added to suggest a winding path through the forest. By sprinkling on a thin layer of peat moss, an illusion of a forest floor may be created. Trees of different heights will establish a sense of reality. An occasional pruning will keep them in bounds.

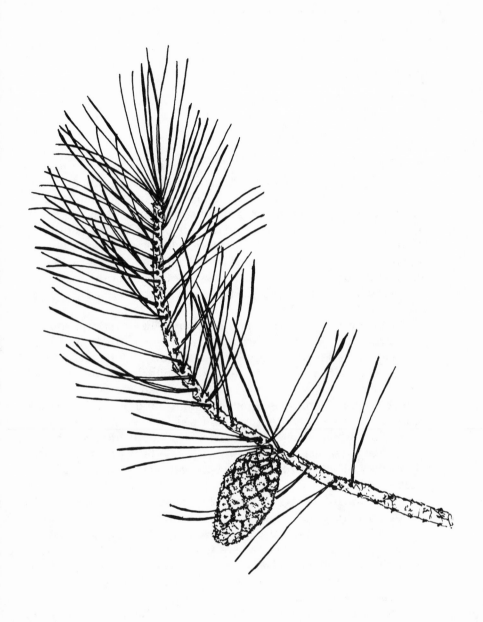

So Hiram gave Solomon cedar trees and fir trees according to all his desire.
(I Kings 5:10)

ALMOND

Amygdalus communis
Biblical term: Almond

YOUNG JEREMIAH WAS CALLED to his prophetic mission during the reign of King Josiah of Judah. He was appointed by the Lord to act as His spokesman, but tried to escape the assignment (Jeremiah 1:6). The Lord, in a dialogue, assured him that He would supply the words. Then, in the first of two visions, Jeremiah looked long at a flowering branch of an almond tree. The first tree to blossom after the winter's sleep, the almond is known as "wakener" or "watcher." To the prophet the branch seemed to be a symbol of an active God who is wakeful and watchful of His word to cause it to be fulfilled (Jeremiah 1:11–12).

The lovely, long-lived almond tree is native to Palestine, Lebanon, and some parts of Mesopotamia, growing either wild or as a cultivated form. Its deciduous leaves are pale green with a grayish tinge. Because of their early bloom, the pinkish-white flowers were to Israel a symbol of hope. Almond blossoms were used as a pattern for the cups on the golden, seven-branched lampstand of the Tabernacle (Exodus 25:32–38), and Aaron's staff was an almond branch which miraculously budded overnight to bear almonds (Numbers 17:5–11). Kernels of bitter-tasting almonds have always been prized for the flavor of their oil and were part of the package sent by Jacob to Egypt (Genesis 43:11).

An almond tree grows rapidly to a height of 15 to 20 feet, usually bearing the first crop of nuts two or three years after planting. Unless a self-pollinating kind is used, however, you must plant at least two varieties to produce fruit. Where late frosts occur, select a late-blooming variety; otherwise, the small fruits that are forming will be destroyed. The tree requires deep, well-drained, sandy soil. Water abundantly but infrequently.

Trees like the almond offer beauty, privacy, and shade as well as welcome crops of delectable fruits. The most essential requirement is a sunny location in the yard. If space is not a problem, an orchard consisting of all the "trees good for food" would provide you with the same splendid fruits enjoyed by Bible-time people.

Almost any type of fruit tree may be cultivated in a container, and the almond is no exception. If the almond is of doubtful winter hardi-

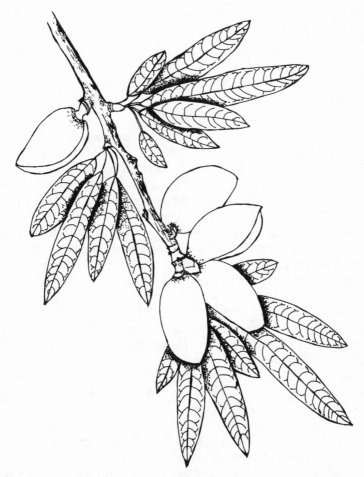

*Moreover the word of the Lord came unto me,
saying, Jeremiah, what seest thou? And I said,
I see the rod of an almond tree.*
(Jeremiah 1:11)

ness outdoors, it can be grown in a large planter box, using a seedling
or a dormant, bareroot specimen. The tree will need daily watering
during the growing season; keep the soil moist at all times. Leave the
plant outdoors most of the year, but winter it over in an interior space
where temperatures do not fall below 20 degrees F.

Although it is an ornamental tree producing no fruit, the dwarf
flowering almond, *Prunus glandulosa,* is closely related to the nut-
bearing tree and could act as a substitute. It is quite hardy, growing
slowly and treelike to 6 feet. Its single pink or white blossoms burst
forth in very early spring.

11

APRICOT

Prunus armeniaca
Biblical term: Apples

THE PREVAILING OPINION AMONG botanical authorities is that the fruit referred to in the original translation of Proverbs 25:11 was the apricot, which was first introduced from Armenia into Palestine during the time of Noah. Apple trees never grew in the Holy Land in biblical times, whereas the apricot still thrives there in valleys and on mountainsides. Proverbs 25:11 gives a perfect description of the golden-orange fruit surrounded by leaves of silvery pale green. Another proof that the apricot was meant appears in The Song of Soloman 2:3, where a tree bearing delicious, sweet fruit is depicted.

The proverb is one of the forms of the many wise sayings attributed to King Solomon and later copied by the men of the court of King Hezekiah of Judah (Proverbs 25:1). Proverbs included in the biblical Wisdom Literature consist of practical advice on ways to attain true success and happiness in everyday situations. In expressive language, Proverbs 25:11 implies that a wise person can improve a personal relationship and brighten a day with a word of kindness, praise, or understanding. It compares such a motive with the loveliness of golden fruit ripening on a tree.

The deciduous, reddish-barked apricot tree grows to 20 feet tall, spreading its branches to a diameter of 20 to 25 feet. Semidwarf trees grow only 12 to 15 feet, making them invaluable where space is limited. A long-lived tree, the apricot begins to produce fruit in its third year. It is a good choice as a fruit, ornamental, or shade tree and grows well in many parts of the United States.

First after the almond to bloom in the spring, the apricot is more susceptible to frost damage in both its masses of soft pink blossoms and its young fruit. Frost damage can be prevented to some extent by planting the tree in a sunny, sheltered location. In very cold areas, choose varieties that grow well where peaches thrive. A deep, well-drained, clay-loam soil is preferable. Water deeply at least once every month in the summer.

An apricot can be easily maintained on a lawn or grouped with other biblical fruit-bearing trees to carry out an orchard theme. A seedling potted singly in a bowl is attractive when trained as a bonsai. Since the seed has an extremely hard coat, it is slow to germinate. Germination is hastened by rubbing the seedcoat with sandpaper for a short time before planting in a container filled with sand.

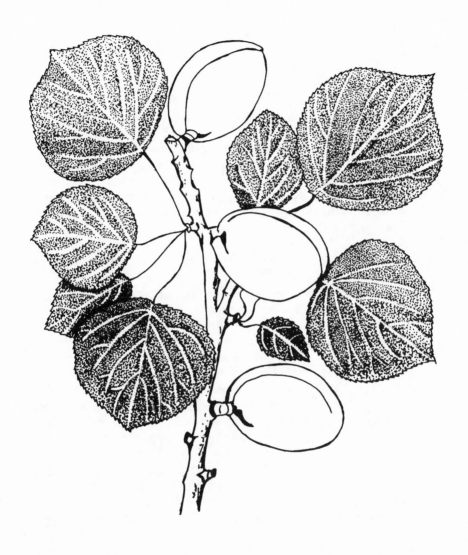

*A word fitly spoken is like apples of gold
in pictures of silver.*
(Proverbs 25:11)

ASPEN

Populus euphratica
Biblical term: Mulberry trees

MOST AUTHORITIES AGREE THAT the mulberry trees mentioned in II Samuel 5:23-24 and in I Chronicles 14:14-15 were actually aspens. This is due to the fact that the fruit-bearing mulberry tree produces soft-textured leaves which have no sound of movement in the wind, while the leafstalk of the quaking aspen is slightly twisted, causing the leaves to rustle in the slightest breeze. Aspens line river and stream banks from Syria to Palestine. In the quoted passage, the leaf movement in the tops of the aspen trees was the signal for David to attack the Philistines.

After David was annointed king of all Israel and had made Jerusalem his capital, the Philistines took action by sending an army into the Valley of Rephaim to stop him from further extending his kingdom. The fertile and productive valley, situated a few miles west of Jerusalem, had often been seized and held by the Philistines. They staged two invasions, but David's army defeated them both times and forced them to withdraw from central Palestine. The Philistines were never again a serious threat to Israel (II Samuel 5:17-25).

The hardy, fast-growing aspen tree rarely reaches a height of more than 50 feet. Its wood is soft, its smooth bark a grayish green. Buds on the twigs are glossy brown and sharply pointed. Male and female flowers appear on separate trees, each in hanging catkins which burst into bloom before the leaves unfold in the spring. Individual flowers are minute and yellowish in color. A similar, closely related form of aspen and more available in the United States, is *P. tremuloides* (quaking aspen). It is a round-headed tree with smooth, grayish-white bark. The attractive, small leaves rustle in the slightest breeze.

Aspens adapt to many types of soils and climates but are partial to moist ground and a sunny location. Although short lived, they are valuable along the sides or back of a lot as a background, divider, or screen. Tall and stately, aspens are unequalled as a border along a driveway or as sentinels by a gate or entrance. A single tree planted on a lawn makes an imposing specimen. Trained as miniatures, a grove of aspens planted in a large bowl would be in keeping with the Scriptural passages. New plants may be started from hardwood cuttings taken in the fall and buried over the winter in sand.

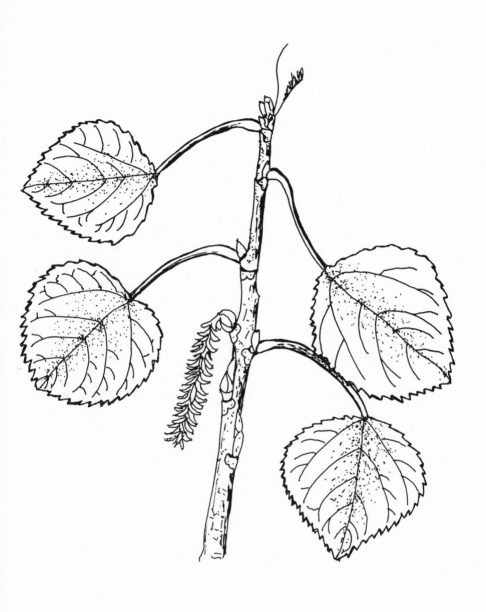

. . . fetch a compass behind them, and come upon them over
against the mulberry trees. And let it be, when thou hearest the
sound of a going in the tops of the mulberry trees, that then
thou shalt bestir thyself.
    (II Samuel 5:23–24)

BALM OF GILEAD

Populus gileadensis
Biblical term: Balm

MANY COMMENTATORS AGREE THAT the "balm" of Jeremiah came from an aromatic gum extracted from a tree which grew abundantly in Old Testament times on the well-watered tablelands of Gilead. Seeds of the sturdy Arabic trees were brought by the queen of Sheba as part of her gift of spices to King Solomon (I Kings 10:19), and the trees continued to exist seventeen centuries after his reign. The city of Gilead was famous for its medicinal balm. Prized for its healing properties (Jeremiah 51:8), balm was exported from Judah to Tyre and Egypt. Jeremiah, while preaching in Jerusalem, predicted the downfall of Judah to Babylonia unless Judah's idol-worshiping people returned to their God, but the people and false prophets only ridiculed his pathetic warnings. In Jeremiah 8:22, the broken-hearted prophet completely expresses his distress concerning Judah's predicted calamities.

Balm of Gilead is a fast growing, spreading tree, esteemed for its large sticky buds, which in springtime have the strong pungent fragrance of balsam. Its somewhat heart-shaped, pointed leaves are golden green, densely hairy on the veins underneath. The stout twigs are angled. Gum or balm was obtained by making incisions in the stems and branches of the trees. The gum was gathered after the yellowish-green sap had hardened into small balls.

While this particular tree no longer grows in Palestine, a similar form also known as balm of Gilead, *P. candicans,* thrives in the United States, the origin of which is in doubt. It is a fast-growing tree from 50 to 60 feet tall, with wide-spreading branches and an irregular, spreading top. Small, greenish-yellow flowers in long, slender catkins appear before the deep green, triangular leaves.

Balm of Gilead tolerates a wide range of soils, requires little water, and is indifferent to unfavorable conditions such as city smoke, dust, and wind. Because its roots are invasive, it suckers profusely and is subject to constant twig drop. The tree serves best at the rear of property where it can offer shade from summer sun and a background for smaller plants. A young specimen may occupy a container to provide a screen for privacy or a background for pots of summer flowers. Propagation is by hardwood cuttings taken in the fall and buried over winter in sand.

Is there no balm in Gilead; is there no physician there?
(Jeremiah 8:22)

BAY, LAUREL

Laurus nobilis
Biblical term: Bay tree

ACCORDING TO TRADITION, DAVID was the principal author of portions of the beloved book of Psalms; Psalms 3 to 41 are attributed to him. The Psalms are composed of prayers expressing praise and thanksgiving from which one can draw encouragement and guidance.

The tall, shrubby bay tree with its wonderfully fragrant evergreen leaves grew infrequently along streams in Palestine. Its pleasing appearance and welcome shade could scarcely fail to attract the attention of a passerby. As David gazed at the tree, its shoots sprouting near the ground at the base, he likened it to people who live in continuous power and great wealth while those about them suffer in despair (Psalms 37:35). To the psalmist the tree symbolized the affluence enjoyed by the wicked. But he points out that by trusting in God the adverse situation would eventually vanish or reverse (Psalms 37:36–40).

In its native Mediterranean area, a bay may reach a height of 60 feet; confined in a 16-inch tub or pot, it grows from 4 to 6 feet tall. The leathery 3 to 4 inch long leaves of dark green are glossy on the upper surface and aromatic when crushed. Small, greenish-white or yellow flowers, borne in clusters, are followed by black or dark purple berries which are about the size of small grapes. The dense foliage, fruits, roots, and bark have long been used in medicine and to add flavor in cookery.

A bay is not particular about soil, but does need good drainage, some water in summer, and protection from frost in most parts of the United States. If possible, bring the plant indoors for the winter; otherwise cover the roots with a heavy mulch. The plant may die back in winter, yet the roots will stay alive. A bay likes morning or afternoon sun, except in extremely hot summer climates where it does best in the dappled shade of a tree. Indoors, place a potted bay plant near a south or east facing window, mist occasionally, and water when the soil surface starts to dry.

A classic formal plant used for ornament, the bay can be trimmed into topiary shapes, standards, globes, and cones. Or place the container as a background for colorful potted biblical flowering plants. Bays may be grown from seed or cuttings. Small plants may be obtained from a nursery.

I have seen the wicked in great power, and spreading himself like a green bay tree.
   (Psalms 37:35)

BOX, BOXWOOD

Buxus sempervirens
Biblical term: Box

THE PROPHET ISAIAH PROCLAIMED that he was sent by God to tell the people of Israel that Jerusalem would be transformed into a holy city and costly woods would be brought from the forests of Lebanon to beautify the temple which had been rebuilt by captives released from Babylon (Isaiah 56–66). The boxwood to be employed in the temple came from a long-lived evergreen shrub or small tree found in dry, hilly regions of Palestine, the Galilean hills, but especially around Lebanon. Its extremely hard, close-grained wood takes an excellent polish and is valued for wood carving. For thousands of years, boxwood was used so extensively in religious ceremonies that it has become nonexistent in many parts of the Holy Land.

Box (boxwood) grows slowly to reach its ultimate height of 10 feet or more. In some of its horticultural forms the plant ranges from a rounded dwarf shrub to a tree 25 feet high. Covered with dense, lively, dark-green foliage, it is considered the best of all plants for hedges or edgings and for clipping into formal shapes.

This pleasing, small-leaved plant is easy to grow in sun or shade, but is subject to snow damage. Form 'Inglis' is recommended for colder areas. Though not fussy as to soils, a little extra care with watering and feeding produces better leaf coloring and strength. Box is propagated by taking hardwood cuttings in early fall or by layering.

A delightful landscape garden can be made by using diminutive replicas of the three trees mentioned in the Bible passage: the cedar of Lebanon, the fir (stone pine), and the box. Fill a concrete or stone container with potting soil and shape the landscape into hills and valleys. After the right place is found for each plant, set them in place. A covering of stone chips will create the setting. Because this type of garden is heavy, it should be planted in its permanent location. A good spot for it is under a high-branched tree where there will be some sun for part of the day. The soil must be kept evenly moist.

*The glory of Lebanon shall come unto thee, the fir tree,
the pine tree, and the box together, to beautify
the place of my sanctuary.*
                        (Isaiah 60:13)

BOXTHORN

Lycium europaeum
Biblical term: Bramble

THE BRAMBLE FIGURES PROMINENTLY in Jotham's famous fable in which the trees choose a bramble for their king (Judges 9:8–15). It is obvious in the rest of the chapter that the fruit trees and vine represent valuable persons such as Gideon's sons who did not seek power, while the spiny, almost worthless bramble represents cruel Abimelech, who was made king after murdering all his half-brothers except Jotham (Judges 9:5).

Several types of brambles grow in Palestine, but the one named in our verse is known today as boxthorn, *Lycium europaeum*. This upright, bushy shrub is native in the Mediterranean region and abounds everywhere in the driest of places. It is used for fuel, hedges, and to feed goats. Ranging from 3 to 6 feet in height, it produces rigid branches with many stout spines. The deciduous leaves are small, narrow, and grayish green in color. It blossoms with small, white or pink, tubular flowers, which are followed by small, oval, edible scarlet berries.

Because of its rank growth and tendency to sucker, boxthorn should be planted in a place where it has plenty of room to spread, far from flower beds. It makes a good covering for steep banks and rail fences or for trailing over rock piles, tree stumps, and unsightly objects. Planted closely, the shrubs become an impenetrable barrier to define property lines.

Boxthorn prefers good drainage but succeeds in any ordinary soil, in sun or shade, and withstands drought and hot winds. It is hardy only in mild climates. A perennial, it grows slowly until well established. Then it may be trained to suit your needs. Propagation is by seeds, hardwood cuttings, or suckers.

Then said all the trees unto the bramble, Come thou,
and reign over us.
    (Judges 9:14)

BUCKTHORN

Rhamnus palaestina
Biblical term: Thorns

TO ADAM AND EVE, THERE CAME from God the threat of unceasing problems in cultivating the soil, including a struggle with pestiferous plants. Difficulties with thorns arising from the ground were acknowledged in David's time (II Samuel 23:6), and in the New Testament thorns continued to express the idea of a worthless nuisance (Matthew 7:16), for they choked out good seed (13:22).

Thorns of many varieties still exist throughout Palestine, Syria, Lebanon, Arabia, and Sinai, advancing over dry, stony places and thickets. In the verse, "thorns" are regarded as referring to the buckthorn, *Rhamnus palaestina*, a spiny shrub or small tree reaching up to 6 feet in height, clothed with oval, evergreen leaves and, in spring, with clusters of inconspicuous flowers which precede the small, black berries. Today the plants furnish food for camels and goats. Desert-walking Bedouins use the prickly branches for a quick-burning fuel.

The genus *Rhamnus* constitutes about one hundred species of buckthorn, largely consisting of shrubs and trees. Common buckthorn, *R. cathertica,* is more attractive than *R. palaestina* and is easier to obtain. Growing from 10 to 20 feet tall, it is a vigorous shrub or, if trained, a single-stemmed tree. Only the old twigs end in spines. The small, oval leaves are lustrous, dark-green, and leathery. Appearing among the leaves in crowded clusters are tiny, greenish, sweet-scented flowers. The glossy black berries, though poisonous to humans, are a source of food for birds. Neither flowers nor fruits are spectacular, but the almost continuous bloom and dense shining foliage make this buckthorn an ideal plant for the biblical garden.

Common buckthorn is tough and hardy in most environments, requiring practically no care. It grows readily in sun or part shade, prefers alkaline soil, withstands drought, heat, wind, as well as regular watering. Easily trimmed to a desired height, it becomes a tall, quick-growing hedge along a fence to give privacy. When trained to a single stem and grown in a large container on a patio, one plant will provide considerable shade. Buckthorn may be propagated from seed, cuttings, or by seedlings.

Thorns also and thistles shall it bring forth to thee.
(Genesis 3:18)

BUTCHER'S BROOM

Ruscus aculeatus
Biblical term: Briers

BEFORE EZEKIEL WAS DEPORTED TO Babylon along with other Israelite captives, God commissioned him to be the mouthpiece of the divine will. In addressing the prophet, God forewarns him that he is being sent to proclaim the message to a hard-hearted and rebellious people (Ezekiel 2:3–5) and compares the expected response to the prophet's endeavors to the painful sting of briers and thorns. In other words, he was called to a life of hardship and persecution. The title "son of man" characterizes him as God's prophet throughout the Book of Ezekiel.

The briers in the Ezekiel passage are believed to refer to what is known to us as butcher's broom, *Ruscus aculeatus.* A prickly, low-growing shrub, it is commonly found in rocky woods in Lebanon and Palestine, particularly around Mount Tabor and Mount Carmel. Often the plant is used for fuel and as a hedge to form a barrier.

This evergreen shrublet grows from 2 to 3 feet high. Its leaflike flattened branches, dull dark green and spine tipped, serve as leaves. The tiny, greenish-white flowers are borne in the center of the thick branches; the marble-sized fruits of bright red or yellow follow the flowers. To produce flowers and fruits, both a male and female plant must be present, unless the single plant is one which bears both male and female flowers.

Spreading by underground runners or stems, the shrublet eventually forms a mat to hold a sloping bank or to prevent weeds from growing. Another species of butcher's broom, *R. hypoglossum*, reaches a height of only 1 1/2 feet, has glossy-green, spineless, leaflike branches. It makes a superior groundcover on rocky and wooded places or under trees where grass is difficult to grow. Because the foliage of butcher's broom retains its stiffness after a thorough air drying, it is frequently dyed brilliant colors for ornamental arrangements. Dipped in a bath of red dye, it provides an element for Christmas decorations. A bundle of butcher's broom in a simple vase can be a tasteful everlasting bouquet.

Butcher's broom does best in a shady location but will survive in full sun, except in desert regions. It adapts to almost any soil and grows successfully indoors in a cool house if the container soil is not too rich. Propagation is by seed, green wood cuttings, or by layering.

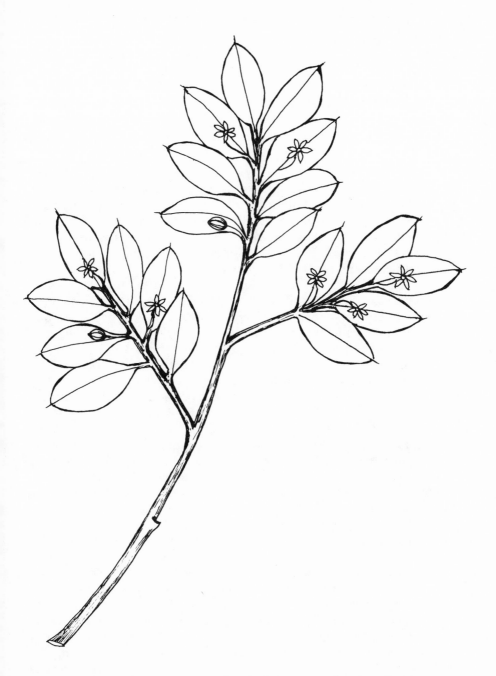

And thou, son of man, be not afraid of them, neither be afraid of their words, though briers and thorns be with thee.

(Ezekiel 2:6)

CAPER

Capparis spinosa
Biblical term: Desire

ECCLESIASTES, THE ENGLISH NAME defined as "The Preacher," was written by Solomon, who reigned as "king over Israel in Jerusalem" (Ecclesiastes 1:1, 12). Authoring the short book in his declining years, Solomon portrays the approach of old age in terms taken from nature (Ecclesiastes 12:5). He measures aging by such signs as loss of faculties and physical decline, thus anticipating the end of man's earthly days and departure to his eternal home.

A great number of authorities feel "caper" is the correct translation for "desire." The Revised Version of the Bible clarifies the meaning of the verse by stating "and the caper shall fail," indicating that even the stimulating effects of the caper can no longer kindle the appetite or senses of an old man dispossessed of his strength. The Preacher's advice to young people is to enjoy their youth, for life is short (12:1). But, he counsels, God will judge you for whatever you do (12:14).

The common caper grows in abundance as a spiny shrub throughout Palestine, Lebanon, Syria, and on the hills surrounding Jerusalem, straggling like a weak vine over ground, rocks, and fissures of old walls. Its large white flowers, borne in the leaf axils on stiff stalks, open in the evening, remain open all night, and wither the next morning. To some the solitary white flower resembles the bowed head of a weary old man ready to depart from the world. The large berries burst when ripe, exposing purple seeds in pale-red flesh.

Capers are the unopened flowers of the caper shrub. During the midsummer flowering season, the young buds are picked in the morning before the petals expand and are preserved in vinegar. The picked buds were used by the ancients, as they are now, for sauces, to add extra flavor to appetizers, meats, seafoods, and salads. Also esteemed in cookery were the elongated berries.

The half-hardy caper, growing to a height of 3 to 6 feet, is suited for planting in the open only in California and Florida. Elsewhere it requires cool, fairly dry winter conditions indoors, with plenty of light. By careful pruning it can be kept within reasonable bounds. Seeds may be sown indoors 8 to 10 weeks before the average date of the last frost and set out when the weather becomes warm. Cuttings of half-ripe wood, potted in equal parts of sand and moist peat moss, form

. . . and desire shall fail: because man goeth to his long home.
(Ecclesiastes 12:5)

roots if kept in a light, warm place and covered with a clear plastic bag.

Grown in a tub as an annual, a caper plant is an attractive flowering shrub for the patio, porch, or balcony. It can also fill a niche in an open spot of your biblical garden.

CAROB, ST. JOHN'S BREAD

Ceratonia siliqua
Biblical term: Husks

WITHOUT QUESTION THE PODS OF THE carob shrub or tree were the "husks" mentioned in Jesus' illuminating parable, in which the youngest son squanders his inheritance and becomes so poor that he eats food ordinarily reserved to fatten livestock (Luke 15:11–32). In Jesus' day, only famished people such as the Prodigal Son resorted to eating carob pods. Many scholars believe the seeds and pulp of the carob were the locusts and wild honey that John the Baptist found in the Jordan wilderness (Matthew 3:4). Hence, the two common plant names are often used interchangeably.

Carobs are distributed widely in Palestine, Syria, and Egypt, being cultivated both for the edible pods and for shade. The pods, up to a foot long and produced most plentifully in April or May, are rich in protein and sugar. They furnish an important forage crop and a nourishing food for the poor of the Near East in times of shortage. Inside the pods are numerous pealike seeds embedded in a mucilaginous and nutritious pulp. When fully ripe the pods turn chocolate brown and fall from the plant. They contain a sweet-tasting, dark-colored syrup, palatable and chocolatelike in flavor.

The evergreen carob grows either as a large shrub or a domed tree, its branches covered with dense, dark-green, glossy, and leathery foliage. If permitted to grow naturally, it retains a bushy form with branches extending to the ground. Trimmed as a tree, with the lower branches removed, it slowly reaches a height and width of 30 to 40 feet. The red flowers of the male carob emit a strong, pungent odor; but to ensure pods, both genders must be planted. The pods—produced by the female carob—are ground commercially into a fine powder for use as a chocolate substitute. The hard, reddish, mature wood is used in cabinetmaking.

Carobs flourish in a warm climate similar to that required by oranges. With some winter protection for the first two or three years, they become less vulnerable to frost. They grow in most types of soils and should be watered deeply but infrequently to prevent root rot. Usually they are reproduced from seed, but they can be raised from cuttings if bottom heat is applied.

While carobs are slow growing, their life expectancy is indeed long.

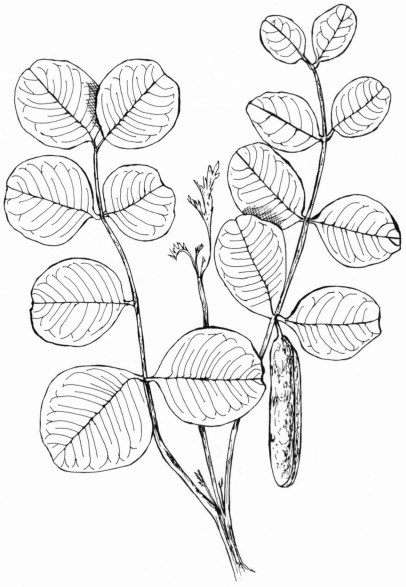

And he would fain have filled his belly with the husks that the swine did eat.
   (Luke 15:16)

To raise as trees, interplant them with other biblical specimens that have a rapid rate of growth. If left in bush form, match them with large-growing biblical hedge plants. One carob can be temporarily grown in a container as a showpiece.

CASSIA-BARK TREE

Cinnamomum cassia
Biblical term: Cassia

CASSIA AND OTHER EXOTIC SPICES were obtained by Solomon through barter with bazaar merchants of the city of Tyre (Ezekiel 27:19), the capital of Phoenicia and a powerful seaport on the Mediterranean. All the treasures and wares of the ancient world appeared in this famous and wealthy city. Included along Tyre's trade routes were Dan, near the head-waters of the Jordan, and the Greek island city of Javan. After the ruin of Judah by the Babylonians, the prophet Ezekiel was given a vision of the downfall of Tyre, and he warns that arrogant center of power and splendor of God's impending judgment (Amos 1:9).

In Palestine the cassia has been known since a remote era, being the source of one of the oldest spices. A native of tropical Asia, the tree grows slowly to a height of 40 feet. Though related and similar to the true cinnamon, the bark of cassia is considered inferior in quality because it is coarser and more pungent. The aromatic spice, secured from the inner bark by making incisions in the branches, was one of the ingredients of the holy anointing oil compounded by Moses (Exodus 30:23–24). When the bark dries and peels, it rolls itself into tubes; these were exported to the Tyre bazaars for bartering. The spicy bark was used in flavoring food and medicine, as well as in preparing delightful, fragrant perfumes (Psalms 45:8).

An evergreen, the cassia tree produces leathery leaves up to 6 inches long that have the smell of cinnamon when crushed. Clusters of tiny, fragrant, yellowish-white flowers appear in profusion during late spring, followed by small, dark berries set in cuplike receptacles. Cassia trees grow outdoors in California and Florida as ornamentals, thriving where summers are hot and temperatures stay above 20 degrees in winter. Elsewhere it must be treated as a half-hardy perennial pot plant. In summer months the plant should be placed outdoors in a sheltered location and in winter brought indoors to a cool, well-lighted room.

Outdoors, the cassia tree does well in a variety of soils, but prefers sandy loam. If used as a pot plant, good potting mix, good drainage, and a nitrogen fertilizer should be provided. It may be propagated by seed or by cuttings of half-ripened wood taken in spring.

Dan also and Javan going to and fro occupied in thy fairs:
bright iron, cassia, and calamus, were in thy market.
                                        (Ezekiel 27:19)

CASTOR-OIL PLANT

Ricinus communis
Biblical term: Gourd

JONAH HAD COME TO NINEVEH AT THE Lord's direction to preach the destruction of that great city if it did not repent. His preaching was effective, and the city was spared, but Jonah was angry at God's mercy. He went outside the city and constructed a booth wherein he sat hoping that the city would still be destroyed (Jonah 3:3–10; 4:1–5). From the Hebrew name of the "gourd" that shaded him from the hot sun, it appears that the plant was really a castor-oil plant.

Since earliest times the castor-oil plant was cultivated by the Hebrews, and the oil from the seed was used to a great extent in their religious ceremonies. The same species of plant is also found in Lebanon and Palestine. In those areas it quickly becomes treelike and bears huge, umbrellalike leaves, making it well suited to spring up overnight and cast shade over Jonah. "So Jonah was exceedingly glad" to have the plant.

Usually grown as a shrublike annual, the castor-oil plant reaches 6 to 15 feet in a season. Where winters are mild, it will live over to succeeding seasons and eventually become quite woody and treelike. The lobed, deep-green leaves are sometimes 1 to 3 feet wide on vigorous plants. Small, reddish flowers, arranged in dense clusters on foot-high stalks, forerun the attractive spiny husks containing the large, shiny, beautifully mottled but poisonous seeds. Both foliage and seeds may cause severe irritation upon contact. The oil from the seeds is the source of castor oil.

Castor-oil plants grow rapidly from seeds planted in May, either where they are to grow or sown indoors in small pots, allowing two or three seeds to each pot. Following germination thin to one plant per pot to avoid overcrowding. Plants need to be moved to larger pots as they grow, and finally they should be planted outdoors. These plants do well in a rich, well-drained, loamy soil, with full sun and plenty of moisture. In a biblical garden a castor-oil plant finds use as a tall screen or as a background in a border.

Where winters are harsh, the false castor-oil plant, *Fatsia japonica*, is an excellent substitute for the true castor-oil plant. It is similar in leaf color and form and can fulfill the same purpose for the biblical garden. Rarely does it reach a height of 10 feet in as many years, usu-

*And the Lord God prepared a gourd, and made it
to come up over Jonah, that it might shadow over his head,
to deliver him from his grief.*

(Jonah 4:6)

ally remaining compact. As a houseplant it needs a good potting soil,
bright light, cool conditions, and yearly repotting while small. Once
the plant is in a 10-inch pot, it can be maintained there for several
years by regular feedings during the growing season.

CEDAR OF LEBANON

Cedrus libani
Biblical term: Cedar

CEDARS OF LEBANON ARE AMONG THE tallest trees, attaining a height of 100 feet or more at maturity in their native habitat. These magnificent cedars grew plentifully on the mountain slopes of Lebanon in Solomon's time and were held in high esteem not only for their beauty and delightful fragrance, but also for the durability of the reddish-colored wood. Solomon, as successor to the throne of his father, David, commissioned King Hiram of Tyre, his trading ally, to supply cedar timbers for the building of the temple at Jerusalem. Noted for their skill in felling trees, Sidonians living along the coast of Phoenicia were employed for the work (I Kings 5:6). The huge timbers were brought down to the coast and floated on rafts to the port city of Joppa, now called Jaffa (I Kings 5:9).

Lebanon was well known to the ancient world for its dense forests of cedar. The wood was preferred above all others for building enterprises, including temples, palaces, and administrative courts. Carried away for centuries, without being replaced, the cedars now are reduced to a few isolated groups located high in the mountains. Yet they show the same attributes as their ancestors. Millions of cedar seeds have been sown in the Lebanon mountains in order to restore the valuable trees. However, the growth rate is slow.

A Lebanon cedar grows to fifteen feet in as many years and in youth is shaped like a narrow pyramid. As it matures, the flat, stiff boughs spread out as wide as the tree's height. The needles that form in tufted clusters are less than an inch long. They are bright green on young trees and dark green on old ones. Egg-shaped, brown cones 4 to 5 inches long appear only when a tree is very old. Bark on the trunk is rough and reddish brown. While the trunk may continue single, it often splits into trunklike branches.

In order to prosper, a cedar tree needs a sunny, open space and prefers a well-drained, loamy soil. Infrequent but deep watering is best. A young tree can be shaped by cutting off the branch tips with hand clippers. Propagation is by seeds sown in the spring or from cuttings of small shoots that sometimes sprout on old wood.

A fine contribution to a biblical garden would be a spreading cedar, which in time turns into a majestic skyline tree. But if you do not have

And therefore command thou that they hew me cedar trees out of Lebanon.
(I Kings 5:6)

space for a towering giant, *Cedrus libani* 'Nana' is a slow-growing variety of the cedar of Lebanon, reaching 15 to 18 feet but more commonly about 3 feet tall. It is exceedingly compact with bright green needles. Planted in a tub it can act as a screen wherever needed, since containerized trees can be moved about. If you are in doubt about hardiness, you can winter the tree under cover.

A deep, 16 to 24 inch container is ideal for preparing a small-scale mountainside scene. The terrain can be built up with pieces of rock covered with soil and tiny cedar seedlings featured high on a leveled area. By leaving a few bare spots here and there and by adding coarse gravel for a groundcover, a realistic effect is achieved.

CHRIST'S THORN, JERUSALEM THORN

Paliurus spina-christi
Biblical term: Thorns

MANY EXPERTS (AND TRADITION) identify the present-day Christ's thorn or Jerusalem thorn as the plant used to make a crown or wreath for Jesus' head as a means of insult and torture. The Jerusalem thorn occurs as an extremely spiny, much-branched, erect shrub in the valleys of northern Palestine and was once common in and around Jerusalem. The flexible, hairy twigs are armed with numerous pairs of needle-sharp, alternately hooked and straight spines. The Roman soldiers braided the manageable branches into a crownlike wreath and placed it on the head of the condemned Jesus (John 19:2).

Christ's thorn is found in dense, impenetrable clumps in the hotter and drier parts of the Mediterranean region to as far as north China. Growing 10 to 20 feet high, the plant has ovalish, leathery leaves that are deeply veined and finely toothed at the margins. From June to July tiny flowers of greenish-yellow bloom in loose clusters, followed by brownish-yellow fruits shaped like miniature umbrellas. Sometimes the plant is used for barrier hedges.

Much easier to obtain than Christ's thorn is the jujuba shrub or tree, *Zizyphus jujuba*, which is similar. It grows at a moderate rate to 30 feet, with flexible, spiny but hairless twigs. The prominently veined leaves are glossy dark green, the small flowers a yellowish color. When ripe the fleshy fruits are a shiny reddish brown to black, oblong or egg-shaped, and about an inch long. Candied and dried, they have a sweet, applelike flavor. The decorative foliage and edible fruits ensure a choice plant for the biblical garden. The jujuba shrub is common around the old city of Jerusalem and may actually have been Christ's crown of thorns.

Both of these deep-rooted shrubs or trees like heat in summer, and neither is hardy north of Washington, D.C. They tolerate drought and alkaline soils, but do best in good garden loam with regular, deep watering. Growing readily in an open, sunny location, they prefer a well-drained soil. Propagation is by seeds sown in the fall or by layering and root cuttings.

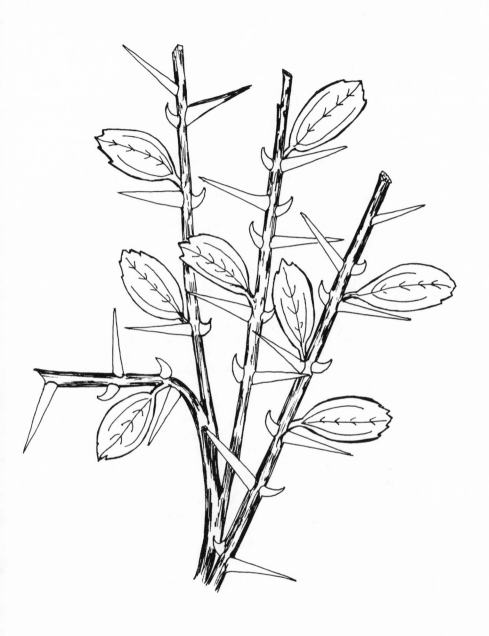

And the soldiers platted a crown of thorns,
and put it on his head.
(John 19:2)

COTTON, LEVANT COTTON

Gossypium herbaceum
Biblical term: Networks

THE HEBREW WORD FOR COTTON IS *karpus* but was translated as "networks" in the King James version of the Bible. Cotton was widely cultivated in Egypt in the time of Isaiah, being used to weave fabrics. In predicting the decline and disintegration of Egypt (Isaiah 19:5–17), the prophet portrays God's judgement on that nation to be manifested in one instance by the drying up of the Nile, whose waters irrigate vast areas of land. Such a calamity would destroy the industry of the workers whose livelihood depended on the processing and weaving of cotton (Isaiah 19:9). Today, as then, cotton is an important commercial crop both in Egypt and Israel.

Levant cotton, assumed to be a native of Asia Minor or Arabia, is one of the earliest of the short-staple kinds to be cultivated. Under tillage the plant is an annual, developing into an erect, finely branching shrub growing up to 8 feet high. Its leaves are heart shaped, lobed, and soft textured. The large, showy blossoms are yellow at first but soon fade to pink or red. Each flower forms a seedball called a boll. When fully ripe, the boll bursts open to reveal the fluffy white cotton attached to the seeds. Collecting the cotton and removing the seeds were performed by hand in the day of Isaiah. Patient spinners and weavers fashioned the fibers into thread and cloth.

While cotton is not generally considered a true garden plant, the Levant type makes a highly ornamental shrub. It is cultivated in the United States commercially wherever there is ample sunshine and water. When its roots are confined to a pot, the growth rate is considerably slower. Pruning will also keep the plant in bounds. The individual, mallowlike flowers bloom in profusion throughout the summer months in areas far north of the cotton belt, but if the bolls are to develop, a great amount of heat is necessary during the growing season.

Levant cotton is easily raised from seed sown early in spring under warm conditions. Move each plant to a larger pot as the plantlets increase in size.

*Moreover they that work in fine flax, and they that weave
networks, shall be confounded.*
(Isaiah 19:9)

CYPRESS (ITALIAN)

Cupressus sempervirens
Biblical term: Cypress

SECOND ISAIAH, A PROPHET WHO lived among the exiles in Babylonia, writes with sarcasm about the absurdity of cutting down trees to manufacture idols (Isaiah 44:14), when it is impossible for man to fashion a true likeness of the one and only matchless God (44:6). The cypress referred to is found in company with the cedar and the oak on Mount Hermon and Mount Lebanon. In the wild it has a wide-spreading crown, whereas cultivated forms are usually columnar. Its fragrant, reddish-colored wood is hard and of great durabilty, making it a desirable material for carving idols.

Also called Italian cypress, this familiar pyramidal form eventually reaches to 60 feet or more. However, it is only 2 to 3 feet in width after twenty to thirty years. The slender branches grow straight upward, well clothed with tiny, dark green, scalelike and aromatic foliage. Even when the trees are quite young, they produce globe-shaped, brown, seed-bearing cones about an inch in diameter. Both the crushed leaves and seeds have been employed in medicine. Often the columnar kinds are planted in cemeteries and against boundary walls for ornament.

Italian cypress is at its best where summers are long, hot, and dry. It readily accepts full sun, deep, sandy loam, and well-drained soil that is kept on the dry side. Though the plant will stand many degrees of frost in a sheltered position, it is wise to cultivate it in a tub in severely cold climates so that the tree can be wintered under cover. It will do well in a peat-based mixture and in a sunny situation in a room. The soil must not be allowed to become waterlogged or too dry.

A miniature forest garden to be kept in the house could include the cedar, the cypress, and the oak mentioned in the Bible verse. Place the container filled with seedlings by a sun-facing window where the plants can receive abundant light. Put the arrangement outdoors during the spring and summer months.

Seedlings can be reproduced by sowing seeds in the spring or by taking cuttings from mature wood in the fall and inserting them in sandy soil. A greenhouselike atmosphere gives the best results.

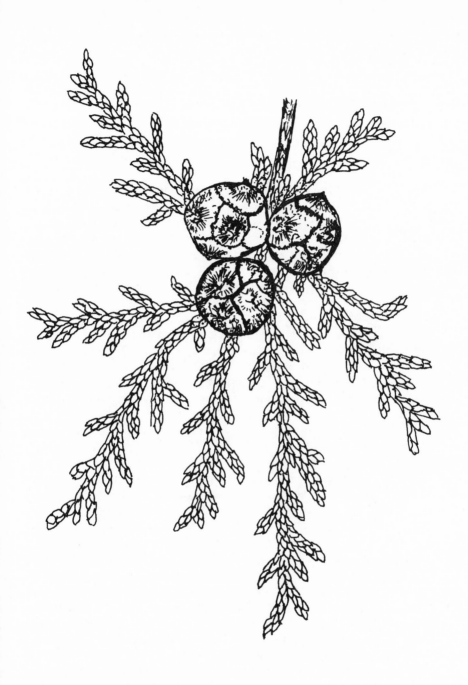

*He heweth him down cedars, and taketh
the cypress and the oak.*
        (Isaiah 44:14)

DATE PALM

Phoenix dactylifera
Biblical term: Palm

AFTER CROSSING THE RED SEA, THE Hebrews reached Elim, their second campsite on the desert. It was a fertile oasis containing seventy palms and twelve springs to supply them with drinkable water (Exodus 15:27). Traditionally, Elim is identified as a wadi sixty-three miles southeast of the present Suez and located on the main caravan route from Egypt to the copper mines of Sinai. To the thirsty wanderers the presence of the tall, immense-headed palms signified that water was available.

Natives of the Middle East, date palms prosper in desert oases, since they require some moisture at their roots and an intensely hot, always dry atmosphere to produce flowers and fruit. The stately trees can be distinguished by their long, slender trunks, topped with crowns of fan-shaped, gray-green leaflets, which are huge, stiff, and sharply pointed. Patterned around the trunks are bases of old leaf stalks, and suckers usually arise from the present bases. Under favorable climatic conditions, small flowers of a yellowish color are borne on long, drooping, branched stalks. They yield large clusters of brown, red, or yellow sweet-tasting dates from June to September.

The date palm can be cultivated in any warm, almost frost-free section of the United States or in a conservatory, but will not bear edible fruit unless it receives the extreme heat of desert regions during April and May. It adapts well to desert and seaside gardens and has survived temperatures as low as 4 degrees F. The leaves are killed by frost at 20 degrees F.

Because these colossal palms soon outgrow their place in a home garden, you can capture some of their spectacular majesty with the pigmy date palm, *P. roebelenii,* a miniature palm with soft, slender, feathery leaves, a medium brown trunk, and of extremely slow growth to about 6 feet. Outdoors it produces flowers and fruits, once out of the juvenile stage. It needs some shade, a rich, fast-draining soil, and moderate watering. A warm, south-facing wall helps it survive when temperatures dip to 28 degrees F. This fine dwarf adapts well to container living, lending itself nicely as a houseplant. After danger from frost has passed, it may be placed outdoors in a shady location until September.

And they came to Elim, where were . . .
threescore and ten palm trees.
(Exodus 15:27)

Unprocessed date palm pits may be sown at any season in a sunny window. Given moisture and a 70 degree temperature, the pits germinate in about two months. Use a large pot when transplanting because the date has a deep root system.

A desert garden planted in a dish could show an oasis with tiny palms, acacias, and tamarisks shading the water holes of Elim. Pockets of potting soil will be necessary to hold the plant roots. An appropriate covering for the nearly flat terrain would be pieces of rugged rock and coarse sand.

DESERT BROOM

Retama raetam (Genista monosperma)
Biblical term: Juniper

THE "JUNIPER" OF THE SCRIPTURAL passage was actually a type of broom, carrying the common names of desert broom, white broom, or bridal veil broom. It grows in abundance as an upright shrub on hillsides, in gullies and rocky places, and on open sandy stretches of the Palestinian desert. Although its leaves are small and sparse, it forms a pleasant shade in desert regions. It was to the secluded desert south of Beersheba that the prophet Elijah fled after Jezebel's threat on his life (I Kings 19:1–7). Under the protective shade of a broom plant, he found a retreat to recuperate from his fears, physical fatigue, and profound depression (I Kings 19:4).

The desert broom grows from 3 to 10 feet in height, with slender, graceful, gray-green, almost leafless branches. Immediately following the rainy season, small clustered masses of sweetly scented white flowers cover the twigs and flaunt a splendid show on the usually barren desert. Like all members of the pea family, the fruit is a long, flattened pod containing several seeds. The thick, deep-growing roots are today, as in ancient times, used for fuel (Psalms 120:4) and the wood from the branches for making charcoal. Even a well-developed broom bush would provide the man of God only a slight degree of relief from the burning desert sun.

Cultivated desert broom rises to 20 feet high, with branches spreading to 10 feet wide. The beautiful sweet-pea-like flowers bloom in late spring and summer. Valued chiefly for its display of flowers, the shrub serves best as a background in a biblical garden or to cover a large, dry bank. To survive it needs mild winters and high summer temperatures. In other areas it should be raised in a pot or tub to be wintered indoors.

Desert broom revels in full sun and a light, impoverished soil that drains fast. Water infrequently in summer. To induce bushiness and free flowering, prune the branches severely right after flowering. Due to its deep root system, it does not transplant well and should not be moved after it has been once established. It can be reproduced by seeds sown in spring under warm conditions or by layering.

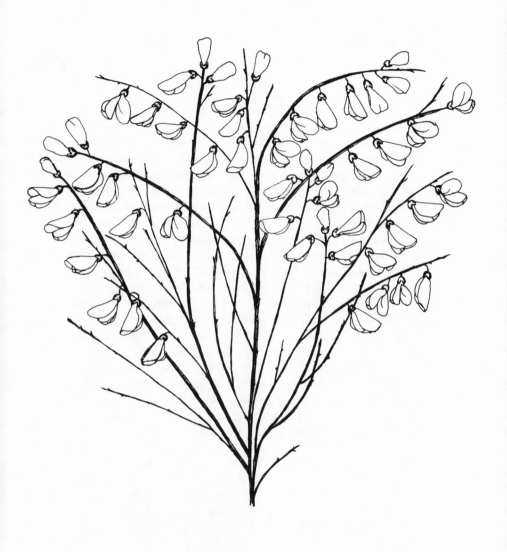

But he himself went a day's journey into the wilderness, and came and sat down under a juniper tree.

(I Kings 19:4)

ENGLISH IVY

Hedera helix
Biblical term: Ivy

THE READING FROM THE APOCRYPHA, II Maccabees 6:7, although not in the King James Version, is found in the Greek and Latin Old Testaments. The ivy mentioned refers to the familiar English ivy, *Hedera helix,* found throughout the world in both temperate and tropical regions. Wild and cultivated forms are found climbing up cliffs, trees, walls, or spreading over the ground in woods and shady places. Ivy has always been linked with religious observances. The ivy leaf was dedicated to the god Bacchus (Dionysus), who in Greek mythology presided over the productivity of nature and wine. Ancient Greeks and Romans wore wreaths of ivy in their hair as a symbol of rejoicing. At the wild and mystic celebrations of Bacchus, Jews of the dispersion were forced to honor the pagan god by marching in processions, either wearing crowns of ivy or holding sprigs (II Maccabees 6:7). Though the Hebrews were subject to much persecution during the period 176 to 161 B.C., their conception of God as the sole ruler remained unchanged. The book of II Maccabees was written in Greek by an unknown author believed to have been an Alexandrian Jew.

English ivy has stout, woody stems and brown aerial rootlets by which it clings to almost any vertical surface. A strong old vine may ascend to 90 feet, transforming a building into an enclosure of foliage. The glossy, leathery, evergreen leaves are stalked and ordinarily have 3 to 5 lobes. On the stiff flowering branches of old vines, the leaves are large and squarish. Mature plants bear small, yellowish-green clusters of flowers near the top of the vine in late fall. They are succeeded by smooth, round, black berries containing 3 to 5 seeds. In the past, English ivy was valued as a medicinal plant.

Where winters and summers are mild, English ivy grows well in sun or shade. In climates with hot summers and cold winters, it needs full shade such as the north side of a house. A moist, humus soil must always be provided. Ivy is easily propagated by cuttings with aerial roots. These may be started in sand or a peat-sand mixture either indoors or out during the growing season.

No other perennial vine can compare with English ivy for beauty, permanence, and hardiness. It is useful as a clinger for fences, walls of buildings, chimneys, the trunks of trees, and for training on decora-

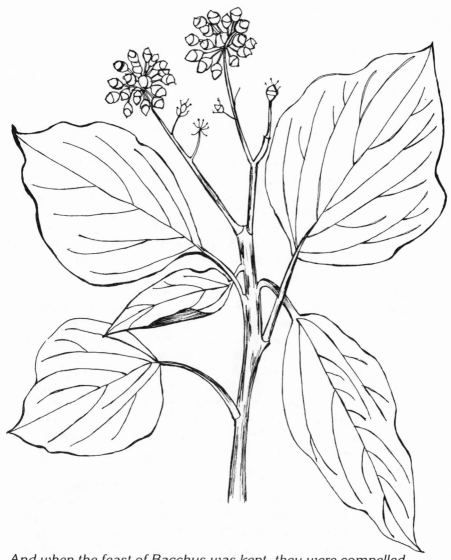

*And when the feast of Bacchus was kept, they were compelled
to go in procession to Bacchus carrying ivy.*
(II Maccabees 6:7)

tive trellises. It is excellent for hanging baskets and window boxes.
Planted 8 inches apart, the vines form a dense carpet under trees
where grass cannot be maintained. The roots grow deep and thick,
making it suitable for holding soil on slopes and steep banks. Indoors, ivy is splendid in pots, planters, or even in a bowl of water.
Wherever used, it will be a wonderful asset to your biblical garden.

FIG

Ficus carica
Biblical term: Fig

WITHOUT QUESTION THE COMMON FIG held an important position in the everyday lives of the ancient Hebrews, mentioned no less than fifty-seven times in the Bible. Fig trees have been plentiful since the dawn of civilization throughout Egypt, Palestine, and Syria, both in the wild and cultivated state, but especially in high-lying areas. Whether spreading vinelike or growing to trees 20 to 30 feet in height, they were prized for their cool shade and flavorful fruits. To acquire a fig tree became the aim of every Hebrew, for it symbolized peace and prosperity. Micah, writer of the Bible book bearing his name, prophesied during the same troubled era as Isaiah. His comforting message of a universal religion, a warless, divinely blessed world of the future (Micah 4:1–3), is pictured in the meaningful illustration, Micah 4:4.

Generally, fig trees in Palestine are not cultivated in orchards, but stand singly or in small groups in private gardens, near wells, and in corners of vineyards, as if claiming status on the landscape. Their longevity is extraordinary, and many produce figs, of brown, purple, green, or nearly black color, several times a year. The second and largest crop usually comes in August or September. Though relished fresh or dried, some figs were reserved for pressing into wholesome cakes (I Samuel 25:18) and for making poultices to heal boils (II Kings 20:7).

Fig trees grow fairly fast, and are generally low branched and spreading. Their trunks are heavy, smooth, gray barked, and knotted when very old. The large, rough, deeply lobed leaves of bright green cast an enjoyable shade in summer. Most varieties bear two crops a year of sweet and juicy fruits, which should be picked as they ripen.

Plenty of summer heat and exemption from long-continued winter cold are the two foremost elements in raising a fig tree. When grown in the open ground, a tree situated as far north as Maryland will develop a crop of fruit, but tub culture is recommended for the coldest of winter climates. A fig tree up to 10 feet in height can be grown in a large container and will winter in a cool cellar or garage. In a colder climate the shoots produced during the previous summer should be protected by covering them with sacking, for it is on these shoots that the fruits form. Pruning should be done in the spring to remove old growth.

*But they shall sit every man under his vine and
under his fig tree.*
    (Micah 4:4)

A fig tree needs a sunny site and good drainage and is not particular about soil. It becomes drought resistant when once established.
To make fruits ripen in cooler climates, give the tree a well-sheltered
situation in the garden, such as next to a wall facing the sun. Training
a tree in a fan shape, or espalier, to grow against a wall, saves space.
The best method of propagation is by taking cuttings in the spring.

GRAPE

Vitis vinifera
Biblical term: Vine

THE GRAPEVINE IS MENTIONED approximately two hundred times throughout the Bible, beginning with the days of Noah to those of Jesus, and is the first plant recorded as having been developed into a crop (Genesis 9:20). In Palestine, the vines are widely cultivated in vineyards for the production of grapes, often on gently sloping land. Because of the close acquaintanceship people had with the activities connected with the cultivation of grapevines, Jesus frequently made reference to them in his parables. A few hours before his arrest, he spoke of himself as "the vine" and his Father as the "husbandman" (John 15:1). His disciples he compared to "the branches." They well understood that the branches of a vine could not bear grapes if the trunk, through which they received nourishment, was cut away (15:5).

An accurate description of a Palestinian vineyard appears in Isaiah 5:1–2, as well as in one of Jesus' parables (Matthew 21:33). By employing pruning hooks, the vines were kept low and weak branches were removed. Harvesting of grapes begins in September, and during this season whole families of villagers move out to the vineyards to work, living in tents or lodges. White grapes are raised for eating out of hand with bread, but the red kinds are dried in the form of raisins or made into a thick, molasseslike syrup by boiling down the juice. For the most part, the grape crop is pressed into juice for a light, sweet-tasting wine. A number of standing Palestinian vineyards have been under cultivation for centuries. Vines sometimes live a hundred years or more without replacement.

Grapevines are strong, woody, deciduous plants, with branches extending from 45 to 60 feet. Their tendrils cling tenaciously to any support within reach. The rounded, 3 to 5 lobed leaves are heart-shaped at the base and often overlapping. When the clustered blossoms appear on long, much-branched stems, they emit a pleasing fragrance. The luscious and healthful fruits, whitish, red, black, or green, ripen from midsummer until late fall, depending upon the variety.

The grapevine of the Bible is the common European species, *Vitis vinifera,* a type of grape with a snug skin and winelike flavor that has high heat requirements in summer. Cold resistance is to 5 degrees F. There are other varieties, however, that grow well with less heat and

I am the vine, ye are the branches.
                    (John 15:5)

that have a cold tolerance to less than zero degrees. Choose a variety
to suit your climate.

One grapevine can yield enough new growth each year to cover an
arch, an arbor, a fence, a trellis, a pagoda, or to shade a deck or terrace. A single young plant placed in a large tub can be kept compact
by allowing the strongest shoot to grow and cutting the others back to
one bud in winter.

For the biblical garden the grape is an excellent choice for shade,
fruit, and ornament. It needs a rich, sandy or loose soil, good drainage, regular pruning, and sun all day. Irrigating the soil when it is almost dry is essential. New plants can be obtained from cuttings.

GREEK JUNIPER

Juniperus excelsa
Biblical term: Algum

THE HEBREW NAME FOR "ALGUM" has been translated in various ways, but commentators recommend the juniper tree, specifically identified as Greek juniper, *Juniperus excelsa,* as the source of the timber imported from Lebanon by King Solomon (II Chronicles 2:8). It grows abundantly in the mountain forests of Lebanon, Syria, and northern areas of Israel, challenging the cedar of Lebanon with its dimensions and attractiveness. Juniper wood was used extensively by Solomon in building the temple at Jerusalem. He received it as part of the cargo from Hiram of Tyre in exchange for agricultural products of his kingdom (I Kings 5:11).

Greek juniper is a slender-branched evergreen that grows to a height of about sixty feet in an upright, spreading form. The bluish-green, needle-shaped leaves on the branches are grouped in threes and have two white bands on the upper sides. Pressed close to the twigs are small, scalelike leaves. Male flowers are borne in small, oval catkins, while the female flowers are composed of little scales, which later develop into purplish-brown, berrylike cones containing four to six seeds. Obtained from the globular cones is an aromatic oil used as a condiment. Wood of the juniper is durable and highly fragrant, well suited for the leaves of the main doors and the flooring in the temple.

Grown as an ornamental plant for its beautiful foliage, the sturdy Greek juniper is conspicuous when planted singly or in groups or as an accent plant in a rock garden. It succeeds in almost any type of soil, but thrives in a sandy and loamy soil with only a moderate amount of water. It also adapts to a somewhat dry, rocky, gravelly type of soil. In hot-summer regions it needs partial shade, while in cool-summer climates it is grown best in full sun or light shade. Propagation is by seeds, which usually germinate the second or third year, or by cuttings of nearly ripened wood taken in the fall and kept under glass or plastic until rooted.

No less beautiful is the spiny Greek juniper of the variety "stricta," growing to 20 feet in height. It has a pyramid shape and produces short, needlelike foliage of gray blue. Though tender, it can be an effective subject in a pot or tub when young, though it should be over-wintered under cover. Small junipers of either kind planted in a wooden box and grouped with tiny cedars of Lebanon and Aleppo pine could be used in creating a delightful biblical alpine scene.

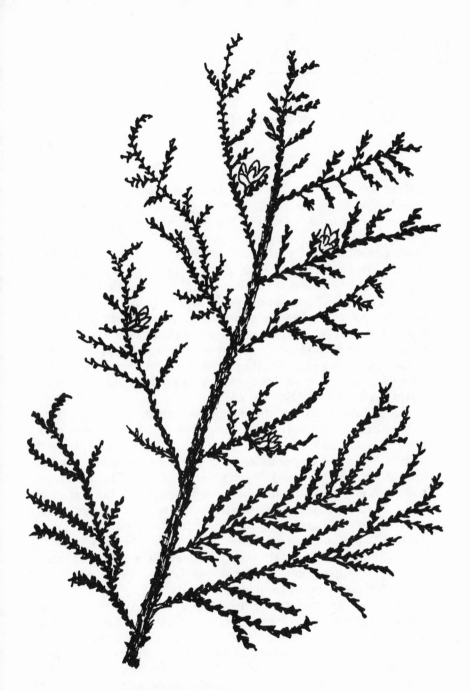

*Send me also cedar trees, fir trees,
and algum trees, out of Lebanon.*
(II Chronicles 2:8)

HENNA PLANT

Lawsonia inermis
Biblical term: Camphire

THE HENNA PLANT, OR MIGNONETTE, *Lawsonia inermis,* is generally acknowledged to be the bush referred to as "camphire" in the King James (Authorized) Version of the Bible. Cultivated since ancient times in the Orient, the plant became naturalized in Egypt, Arabia, Syria, Lebanon, and Palestine. In the Bible reference the Shulamite maiden, the bride-to-be, speaks of her shepherd lover as resembling the clustered blossoms on a henna plant concentrated in the vineyards of En-gedi (Song of Solomon 1:14). En-gedi is the name of an oasis fed by warm, freshwater springs, situated midway along the western shores of the Dead Sea. Waters tumbling over a cliff supplied En-gedi with a handsome growth of semitropical plants. Henna bushes and spices sustained the people there, probably as early as the days of Solomon. It was in the bordering gorges and ravines that David hid from Saul (I Samuel 23:29).

Henna flowers have a strong fragrance much favored by Middle Eastern people. Women arrange them in their hair, wear them in their clothing, and fashion them into bouquets. Liquid distilled from the flowers is applied as perfume. Since remote ages henna has been used as a cosmetic among Egyptians and Hebrews. The dried leaves and twigs are crushed into a fine powder, mixed in hot water, and made into an orange-red paste to be spread over various parts of the body, including fingernails, palms of the hands, toenails, and soles of the feet. Beards and hair were tinted with henna. The dye was washed off the following day, but the stain remained three or four weeks. After that, the applications were renewed. Today henna paste is used chiefly for dyeing fabrics and leather goods.

The woody henna forms a slender plant 8 to 10 feet tall. When young the shrubs are spineless, while on older plants the branchlets harden into spines. The short stalked, smooth, pale green leaves are more or less lance shaped and about an inch long. At the tips of the branches are loose clusters of small, sweet-scented, creamy white, sometimes rose-pink or red, four-petaled flowers. When the plant is grown for commercial purposes, the young branches are first cut when the plant is three years old and twice a year thereafter.

A henna plant can be grown outdoors with success only where win-

My beloved is unto me as a cluster of camphire
in the vineyards of En-gedi.
    (Song of Solomon 1:14)

ters are mild, for example in Southern California and Florida. There the plants abound as ornamentals, prized for their lovely, sweetly scented flowers. The needed environment may be created elsewhere by maintaining a single plant in a pot and transplanting it to larger containers as it grows. To do well indoors, a henna plant requires bright light, a temperature of not less than 65 degrees F., moist air, and a vacation outdoors on a patio or terrace in warm weather. This biblical plant is rather rare in this country but well worth a search for seeds or cuttings.

HOLLY OAK, HOLM OAK

Quercus ilex
Biblical term: Oak

MOST AUTHORITIES AGREE THAT the oak associated with the patriarch Jacob was the noble holly or holm oak, a venerated tree connected with important Bible events and people. This tree once dotted the mountainsides of Mount Carmel and Tabor, and formed groves on the hot slopes of Ephraim, but through the centuries the trees were cut down for fuel, shipbuilding, furniture, tools and other articles. Jacob, on his journey to Bethel (Genesis 35:1–10), took all the family idols and jewelry of his household and hid them beneath a holly oak (35:4). Later, at Bethel, a stone slab was erected under a holly oak to mark the grave of Deborah, the faithful nurse of Rebekah (35:8).

The stately, evergreen holly oak grows 2 to 4 feet a year when young and becomes 40 to 60 feet tall in twenty-five to fifty years. However, it is often encountered as a low shrub. In spite of its rapid growth, it often lives for several centuries. Its small leaves are deep green above, gray and hairy beneath, and vary in size and shape. Their margins may be prickly and hollylike, particularly on young suckering shoots. In late spring the flowers are borne in slender, pendulous catkins. The oval shaped acorns, about one-half inch in length, are embraced by cups covered with gray-haired scales. When fully ripe, the acorns deepen to a shining chocolate brown and are used as food by some animals. The wood of the massive trunk and the stout, wide-spreading branches is hard, tough, and durable. In ancient times, it was used for houses and shipbuilding. The bark was used for dyeing and tanning leather.

As a native of southern Europe, holly oak will not tolerate prolonged, chilling winters, nor temperatures below 30 to 40 degrees F. Considerable protection is needed in colder regions. Elsewhere, the tree requires a sunny location where advantage can be taken of the shade it casts. It adapts to any soil, but responds well to rich soil and regular feedings. Fairly constant and deep watering helps promote growth. Propagation is usually by acorns, which are planted three to a pot in a potting mix as soon as gathered in the fall. Later it is advisable to reduce the seedlings to one in each pot.

The combination of beautiful thick foliage, permanence, strength, and rugged individuality makes this oak a superior ornamental and

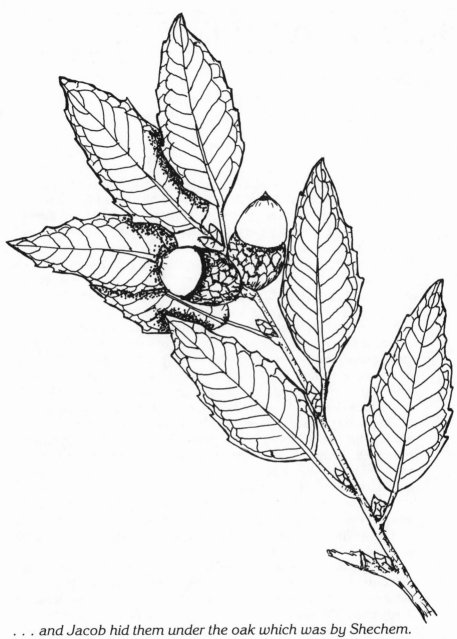

. . . and Jacob hid them under the oak which was by Shechem.
(Genesis 35:4)

shade tree. Its deep root system does not compete with other plants for food and water, thereby permitting smaller plants to grow beneath its branches.

JUDAS TREE, REDBUD

Cercis siliquastrum
Biblical reference: "hanged himself"

AFTER THE PRIESTLY OFFICIALS refused to accept the thirty pieces of silver from Judas Iscariot (Matthew 27:3–4), he hurried to the temple area, threw the betrayal money on the floor, and hanged himself (27:5). The Matthew passage does not indicate that Judas hanged himself from a tree, yet according to well-established legends it was from a tree now known as Judas or redbud, *Cercis siliquastrum*. For more than two hundred years this plant has been recognized as "Judas tree." A native of Eurasia, it is common in the wild on rocky slopes and along borders of streams in Palestine.

Early herbalists frequently featured the Judas tree. One surviving woodcut shows the figure of Judas Iscariot suspended from a limb, clearly revealing the popular belief regarding the legend. Traditional lore associates the color of the flowers with the shame they suffered when Judas selected their beautiful tree for suicide. Through the years Judas has been greatly despised for his betrayal of Christ.

This slender graceful tree, growing to about 30 feet in height, is among the first to bloom in the spring. Then its leafless, spreading branches, twigs, and sometimes even the main trunk become crowded with brilliant, rose-purple, sweet-pea-like flowers all borne in small clusters. After the blossoms start to fade, the rounded leaves emerge, eventually reaching 3 to 5 inches in size. Heart-shaped at the base and of a dark green color, the leaves exhibit fall color with the first frost. The flowers are replaced by clusters of flat, red-purple pods nearly 4 inches in length.

The warmth-loving Judas tree requires protection in the coldest winter regions and is occasionally damaged by late frosts. A good substitute for it is the American redbud, *Cercis canadensis,* which is hardy everywhere. Both species are easily cultivated in a light, rich, loamy, not too moist soil, in either full sun or under the shade of a large tree. Like all *Cercis,* they prefer spring planting and are best transplanted in the spring. Propagation is by seeds sown in spring, by layering, or by greenwood cuttings taken in early spring.

Because of its early, spectacular blossoms, the Judas tree is useful for color in the shrubbery while most other deciduous plants remain

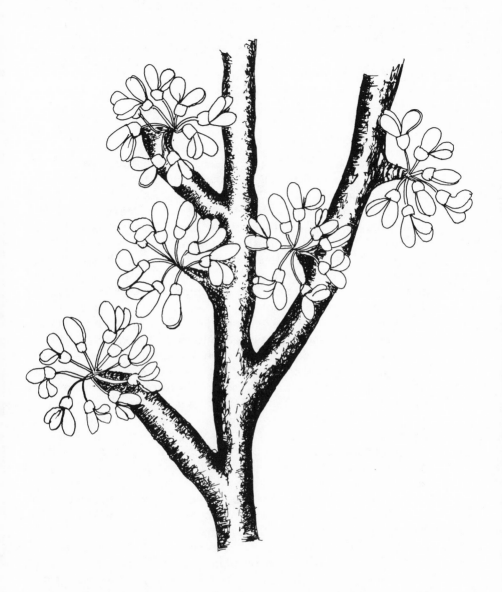

And he cast down the pieces of silver in the temple, and
departed, and went and hanged himself.
(Matthew 27:5)

dormant. Its size affords it a place in a small garden, on an open patio
or terrace, or as a specimen on a lawn. As table decorations the flowering branches are unequalled for beauty.

MULBERRY

Morus nigra
Biblical term: Sycamine tree

THE SYCAMINE TREE MENTIONED by Jesus to his disciples was actually the black mulberry, *Morus nigra*. A native of western Asia, it has been cultivated for centuries in Palestine, mainly for its delectable fruit which is often combined with honey, sugar, and spices to make a popular drink. For the greater part of the year these small shapely trees capture the eye with their fresh greenness. Their dense summer foliage cools the earth and offers a haven for birds. When Jesus' disciples exclaimed "Lord, increase our faith" (Luke 17:5), he illustrated the power of faith by contrasting the tiny mustard seed (Matthew 13:32) with the sturdy mulberry tree.

Black mulberry is a thick-crowned, stiff-branched tree growing to 30 feet in height and has a short, stout trunk. The large, deciduous, dark green leaves, rough above and hairy beneath, taper to a point. Small greenish heads or spikelets of flowers precede the large, fleshy, black or dark red fruit, which resembles a raspberry in appearance. Birds are exceedingly fond of them. When fully ripe, the fruit is shaken from the tree onto a sheet or straw and can be used for piemaking.

Winter hardy, the black mulberry likes full sun and grows rapidly in hot climates. Growth is slower where the weather is cool. It performs best in a rich, deep soil, but any average soil will do. Though it will tolerate some drought once established, the tree grows faster with regular watering and feeding. Propagation is by seeds sown in late January or early February, by cuttings, or by layering.

It is possible for a housebound gardener to grow a biblical mulberry in a pot on a windowsill when the plant is small. Even if called a tree, it is suitable as a houseplant because of its ability to tolerate the dry, static conditions inside a home. Good light is recommended—an east or west window. Let the soil dry out between irrigations. As the tree grows, its size will be limited only by the height of the ceiling. After outgrowing its indoor home, the mulberry may be moved outside to stand in its tub on a patio, or used to fill a landscape niche in a garden.

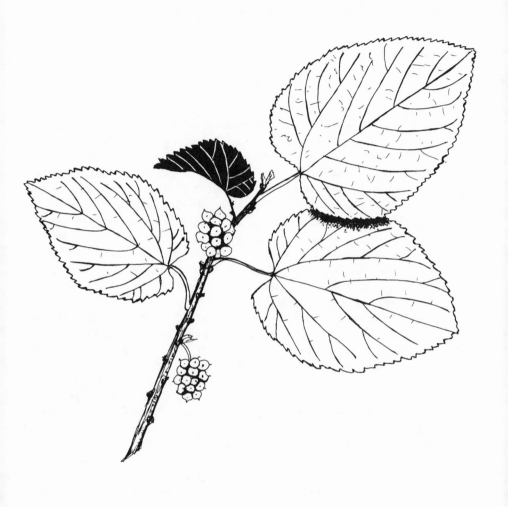

If ye had faith as a grain of mustard seed, ye might say unto this sycamine tree, Be thou plucked up by the root, and be thou planted in the sea; and it should obey you.

(Luke 17:6)

MYRTLE

Myrtus communis
Biblical term: Myrtle trees

A NATIVE OF THE MEDITERRANEAN region and western Asia, the evergreen myrtle is common in Palestine and Lebanon, as well as on the slopes of Mount Carmel and Mount Tabor. It grows in the Jerusalem area as it did at the time of the recording of Zechariah's prophecies. The passage (Zechariah 1:8) is the first of a series of messages the prophet and priest Zechariah received through an angel of the Lord during the reign of Darius (1:1), a Persian king favorably inclined toward the Hebrews, who had mandated that the Jerusalem temple be restored. In the vision the horsemen patrolling the earth report to the angel who was standing among the myrtles that all "is at rest" (1:11). This suggests the peace and quiet prevailing throughout the Persian Empire. God's word, by means of Zechariah, is intended to rebuild confidence and hope in the Hebrews.

Old myrtles can reach treelike proportions of 15 feet in height, but in youth they are likely to be rounded shrubs 5 to 6 feet tall. Their wood is hard, fine-grained, and mottled, and the branches are often gnarled. The small, pointed, bright green, almost stalkless leaves are leathery and impart a delicate aroma when bruised. In summer the scented white flowers with numerous projecting stamens decorate the shining foliage with their blooms. They are followed in the fall by rounded, black or bluish-black, edible berries. Leaves, flowers, and berries are rich in an aromatic oil used in making perfumes and sachet powders. The bark and roots are employed for tanning leather. Branches of myrtle were used to adorn the temporary huts during the Festival of Booths (Nehemiah 8:14, 15). To the Hebrews the myrtle was a symbol of peace and justice.

Half-hardy perennials, myrtles tolerate drought and heat. Whether located in the sun or light shade, they will thrive in almost any soil as long as it is well drained. For protection against frost, place them against buildings or walls. In northern areas, myrtles can be grown in pots for window or room decoration. A myrtle confined in a pot will have a spread and height of about 2 or 3 feet, and careful trimming will reveal the interesting branch structure. The hard seeds require three months of stratification before being sown in September or October. Readily propagated are partially ripened cuttings taken from July to September.

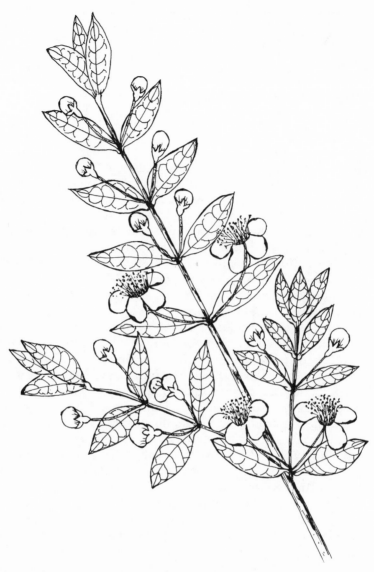

I saw by night, and behold a man riding upon a red horse, and he stood among the myrtle trees that were in the bottom.

(Zechariah 1:8)

Myrtles are widely grown for their exquisite flowers, glistening year-round foliage, and edible berries. Outdoors they are valued as hedges and screens to provide privacy or to act as dividers between different areas. They become outstanding when displayed as single specimens, either in the ground or in pots.

OLEANDER

Nerium oleander
Biblical term: Rose

TODAY THE MAJORITY OF SCHOLARS accept the "rose" of Ecclesiasticus 24:14 and 39:13 as the common oleander, sometimes called rosebay, for it is believed to have been present in Palestine during the time (180 B.C.) when the passages were written. A native of southern Europe and northern Africa, it became naturalized throughout the tropical and subtropical world. Now it grows as an evergreen shrub and is a permanent source of admiration in Palestine, lining watercourses and wadies in great profusion. Oleander is found in quantities around the lakes of Galilee and Tiberias, beside the banks of the Jordan River, and along the brooks pouring into the Dead Sea.

Ecclesiasticus, originally written by Jewish authors, was omitted from the Protestant Scriptures, but is fully represented in the Latin Vulgate and preserved in the Greek Bible. In the passage 39:13, the sage adviser uses an illustration from nature to guide the earlier years of youth. He implies that just as a bud swirls open in all its fresh loveliness and purity, so should God's children be holy and unblemished.

Oleander is an outstanding shrub reaching a maximum height and width of 5 to 12 feet. Its leathery, narrow, glossy, dark green leaves remain attractive at all seasons. It is highly valued for the multitude of flowers borne in dense clusters at the ends of its branches, forming a splendid display from early summer until midfall. The flowers, 2 to 3 inches across, range from pure white to shades of pink, salmon, and red, with some varieties radiating fragrance. Included are kinds with double and single flowers, the doubles appearing roselike in structure.

Though the oleander survives in almost any soil and can withstand considerable drought and poor drainage, it responds with a wealth of flowers under better treatment. Full sun assures strong growth. In cold climates, this tender perennial must be cultivated in a large pot or tub so it can be wintered indoors in a cool room by a window with much sunlight. The oleander is propagated by seed, by cuttings placed in water, or by cuttings set in sandy soil between December and March. Since the plant contains a poisonous juice, children should be cautioned against nibbling any of the parts.

The oleander makes a showy subject outdoors as a lawn specimen,

Hearken unto me, ye holy children, and bud forth as a rose growing by the brook of the field.
            (Ecclesiasticus 39:13)

a hedge, or a screen. It can be pruned drastically in early spring and is easily trained into a small tree. Grown in a container, it will bloom the entire summer on a patio or by a doorway.

OLEASTER, RUSSIAN OLIVE

Elaeagnus angustifolia
Biblical term: Oil tree

IT IS BELIEVED BY MANY AUTHORITIES that the "oil tree" referred to in the Isaiah verse is the oleaster, also known as Russian olive, *Elaeagnus angustifolia*. Growing as a small tree, it is native to Eurasia and is found around the stony hills of Samaria, Mount Hebron, and Mount Tabor. The thorny plant is utilized for hedges in the Palestine region, and the olive-shaped fruit produces an oil which is employed as a medication. God, speaking through the lips of Isaiah, promises that the oleaster tree, among others, will grace the wilderness in the days ahead (Isaiah 41:19). Living with the Jewish exiles in Babylon, Isaiah's exalted messages voiced comfort and hope for better times under Persian rule (44:28, 45:1).

Under favorable conditions the oleaster tree grows rapidly to reach a height of 20 feet. Its dark brown bark has a shaggy or shredded semblance, while the trunk sometimes exhibits a twisted shape. Its graceful branches (often thorny) are thickly clad with deciduous leaves, grayish-green above, silvery and scaly beneath. As the long, slender leaves flutter in the wind, they have a silvery appearance. Extremely fragrant, tiny, greenish-yellow flowers cluster in the leaf axils in early summer, their petals silver-haired on the outer surface and yellow beneath. In the fall appear numerous small, egg-shaped, silver-gray or yellow, nutlike fruits that remain on the tree almost all winter. The flesh is sweet but decidedly mealy. The fruits are at times dried, pounded, and made into cakes. The wood of the tree is hard and fine grained.

Oleaster is hardy, easily grown, and indifferent to wind and heat. It grows in almost any well-drained soil and adapts to a wide variety of dry situations. It prefers a sunny site and is apt to perform poorly in mild-winter, cool-summer climates. Propagation is by stratified seeds sown the second season, or more readily by cuttings of mature and half-ripened wood, by layers, and by root cuttings.

Being of dense growth and wind resistant, oleaster acts well as a screen or windbreak. Tending to produce low branches, it can be trimmed as a medium-height hedge. Sprays of the glistening, silvery leaves are used for dried flower arrangements.

A small-scale desert landscape exhibiting the trees named in the

*I will plant in the wilderness the cedar, the shittah tree, and the
myrtle, and the oil tree.*
> (Isaiah 41:19)

passage would serve as a reminder of Isaiah's promise that no matter
how unworthy His people are, God is near to help them. Start with a
shallow container filled with a moist potting mix. Add a few rocks,
positioned so they will appear partly buried when the scene is com-
pleted. The seedlings of various heights are set among the rocks. A
layer of coarse sand spread between plants and rocks will give a des-
ertlike appearance.

OLIVE

Olea europaea
Biblical term: Olive tree

THE COMMON OLIVE WAS ONE OF the most serviceable trees in Palestine and has played an important role in its history. It was cultivated primarily for the oil from its fruits. Moses called Canaan a "land of oil olive" (Deuteronomy 8:8); Ezekiel and Hosea mention the exportation of the oil to other lands (Ezekiel 27:17; Hosea 12:1). The tree's greenness throughout the year has always been appreciated, the spreading branches supplying shelter from the sun during the scorching days of summer. Branches of the tree have been thought of as an emblem of peace since the days of Noah and its oil as a symbol of abundance. David contrasts his righteousness with the beauty and strength of the olive tree (Psalms 2:8). He is confident that God will deliver him from his wicked, boastful enemy, Doeg the Edomite (I Samuel 21:1–22:18). This beautiful psalm of faith, attributed to David, was used in Hebrew musical worship.

In Palestine practically every village has its olive grove or orchard, the trees thriving in the rocky, parched terrain with little care, living and bearing fruit for centuries. Fresh or processed, the fruit is eaten along with bread as a staple part of the diet. In Bible times oil of the fruit was squeezed out with the feet (Micah 6:15). It was used for a variety of purposes: for cooking, light for lamps, ointments for the hair, and to anoint the body during religious ceremonies. In New Testament days, the oil was used for healing the sick (Mark 6:13). Olive oil is valued today for cooking, soapmaking, and in medicine. The hard, strongly grained wood is useful for carving and cabinet work.

Olive trees are slow growing, finally reaching 25 to 30 feet in height and width. Their willowlike leaves of soft gray-green are offset by the silvery sheen on the undersides. Smooth gray trunks of the early years become knotted and picturesque with age. Clusters of tiny, white, fragrant flowers stud the trees in summer, borne on the growth of the previous year. The small, round fruits ripen in late fall, the color then ranging from reddish-purple to black. The raw fruit has a bitter taste and is not palatable to Western people until processed.

An olive tree will grow in alkaline, shallow, or stony soil, but to produce large-size fruits, deep, rich soil with some fertilizer is required. Drought conditions cause no problems, although hot summers are

But I am like a green olive tree in the house of God: I trust in the mercy of God for ever and ever.
(Psalms 52:8)

essential for fruit bearing. Injury to the tree occurs at 15 degrees F. and to the fruit at 28 degrees F. For propagation, use either hardwood or softwood tip cuttings.

Noteworthy for its decorative foliage and blossoms, an olive tree is highly desirable in a biblical garden if the climate is right. Moderately severe pruning each year exposes the rustic branch patterns to the greatest advantage. A young olive tree makes a pleasing house plant and will bear flowers when offered four or more hours of sunlight daily. It does well at average house temperatures and if the soil is permitted to remain somewhat dry between waterings.

PISTACHIO

Pistacia vera
Biblical term: Nuts

MOST COMMENTATORS GRANT THAT the "nuts" sent as a gift by Jacob to the ruler of Egypt were pistachio nuts (Genesis 43:11). The tree is believed to have originated in Syria and is found growing wild in stony areas of Lebanon and Palestine. For centuries it has been cultivated in Palestine for its fruits, which are prized for the sweet, mellow flavor of the kernels, which are eaten raw or fried and constitute a choice dessert. Sometimes the kernels are pressed into oil, while ground kernels are commonly used for coloring and flavoring confectionery. At the time of a great drought, Jacob knew there was grain in Egypt (Genesis 42:1–3). Knowing the Egyptians relished the products of Canaan, he included pistachio nuts among his gifts.

The deciduous gray-stemmed pistachio tree has broad-spreading branches, yet rarely attains a height of more than 30 feet. Its leaves are wide, thick, leathery, oval, gray-green in color, and taper at the base. The small inconspicuous male and female flowers, blooming in clusters, appear on separate trees. Nuts of the pistachio form in heavy clusters, each egg-shaped, hard-shelled nut being about an inch long. When ripe they are hulled and dried. The kernels, or seeds, are rich and oily, and are pale green to creamy white in color. In this country the mild-flavored nutmeats are enjoyed for out-of-hand nibbling, as well as to add color and flavor to candies, cakes, desserts, ice creams, and breads. A large amount of these delicious nuts are imported from the eastern Mediterranean region and are also harvested in Arizona, California, New Mexico, and Texas. Sometimes a red food dye is added when the nuts are salted and mechanically roasted.

Pistachio trees prosper in regions suited to the olive, reveling in dry summer heat. They reach maturity after ten years. Though not fussy as to soil type, they do need excellent drainage and sunshine. Established trees can survive considerable drought. Young trees should be staked to prevent drooping and their limbs pruned regularly to develop good structures. Seeds of the pistachio should be soaked overnight in lye water before starting them in the house in March. Or the plant can be propagated by budding and grafting.

In a favorable climate, this small tree has the advantage of delivering fresh, tasteful nuts and handsome foliage to enhance the garden

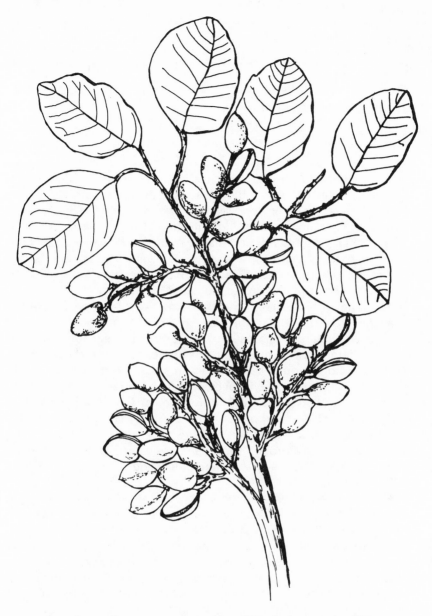

. . . carry down the man a present, a little balm, and a little honey, spices and myrrh, nuts, and almonds.
(Genesis 43:11)

landscape. A male tree must be included in the planting if the female is to bear fruit. One of each kind would be appropriate in a biblical orchard.

PLANE

Platanus orientalis
Biblical term: Chestnut tree

THE PLANT REPRESENTED AS THE "chestnut tree" in the King James Version is accepted by most authorities as the plane tree, *Platanus orientalis,* which is prevalent along riverbanks and streams of Syria and to a lesser extent in Lebanon and Palestine. This is a large tree that grows in the bottomlands and marshy places. All year its older bark sheds in patches, exposing a smooth, pale yellow inner bark. By the use of the rods described in Genesis 30:37, Jacob was able to outwit Laban, his father-in-law, and to increase his own flocks at Laban's expense. The bark of a real "chestnut" tree would not peel as would branches from the poplar, the hazel, or the plane.

The deciduous plane is fast growing, ultimately reaching 60 feet or more in height, with a massive trunk sometimes 30 feet in girth. Its colorfully mottled outer bark is an interesting feature the year round. Large, broad, bright green leaves, with 5 to 7 lobes and long stalks, form a dense head of foliage. Minute greenish flowers appear in ball-like, stalked, clusters, with the female clusters maturing into masses of small nutlets. Even after drying, the brown nuts continue to hang from the branches through winter and are valued in flower arrangements. The wood takes an excellent polish and is therefore prized by cabinetmakers.

A true plane tree of the *orientalis* species is rarely encountered in the United States. What is usually offered as a plane tree by nurserymen is the similar London plane, *P. acerifolia,* a tall, broad, spreading tree with silvery white, flaking outer bark. Both species tolerate an extensive range of growing conditions such as poor soil, drought, neglect, smog, soot, dust, heat, and cold. They are strong, persistent, break resistant, and hardy everywhere. Propagation is by seeds sown in spring or by cuttings of ripened wood.

A plane tree is unsurpassed to give a quick landscaping effect to the biblical garden. It is splendid as a lawn or street tree for beauty and shade. Smaller-growing flowering shrubs and trees can be planted beneath the branches, due to its open structure. For example, combine it with the Judas tree and myrtle.

And Jacob took him rods of green poplar,
and the hazel and chestnut tree.
            (Genesis 30:37)

POMEGRANATE

Punica granatum
Biblical term: Pomegranates

THE POMEGRANATE HAS BEEN UNDER cultivation in Egypt and Palestine from time immemorial, producing one of the favorite fruits in those lands. The Israelites thoroughly enjoyed the refreshing, tangy fruit during their years of slavery in Egypt, and pomegranates were brought from Canaan by Israelite spies (Numbers 13:23). As they followed Moses through parched deserts, the Israelites complained about the lack of pomegranates (20:5). At a later date, King Solomon developed his own orchard of pomegranates (Song of Solomon 4:13). The fruit was eaten out of hand and the juicy pink pulp was made into cooling beverages and sherbets. Pomegranates inspired artwork for adorning the Jerusalem Temple (I Kings 7:20) and for decorating the robes of the high priest (Exodus 39:24). Coins issued in Jerusalem were stamped with depictions of the beautiful blooms.

Growing as a deciduous shrub or small tree, a pomegranate attains a height of 10 to 20 feet. Its often spiny branches bear narrow, glossy, bright green leaves that turn brilliant yellow before falling. For several weeks in late spring, small clusters of flaming orange-red flowers show in the leaf axils. The apple-shaped, burnished, red fruits ripen in the fall, their inner pulp improving in taste the longer they hang on the tree. Within the tough outer skin are countless segments full of juice, each containing a tiny seed. Yielding a sweet, slightly acid flavor, the juice ranks high in warm, dry parts of the world. A red dye was made from the flowers and the outer skin of the unripened fruit. The bark, rind, and root were once used in medicine.

A pomegranate tree grows well in almost any soil with good drainage, but requires full sun and deep and regular watering for best blooms and quality fruit. Winter temperatures must stay above 10 to 15 degrees F. Where a climate does not qualify, or space is limited, the dwarf pomegranate, *P. granatum* "Nana," is best. This is a dense, compact, small-leaved shrub growing to 3 feet tall, making it an ideal container plant. Its flashy, orange-red blossoms are followed by small, red, edible fruits. When exposed to strong sunlight, the fruit ripens enough to eat. Water the plant well in summer, and protect it from frost in winter. Either type of pomegranate may be propagated by seed sown in January or February, by using suckers that spring up around the tree base, or by cuttings of dormant wood.

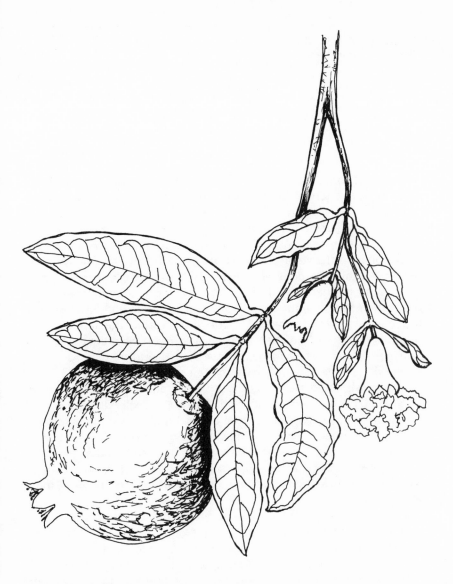

. . . it is no place of seed, or of figs, or of vines,
or of pomegranates.
    (Numbers 20:5)

A pomegranate tree may be trained to have a single or multiple trunk or it can be treated like a vine and trained in a flat pattern to decorate a trellis. Used as showy hedge plants, pomegranates will form dense barriers or screens that need little or no pruning. Dwarf pomegranates in mild climates make desirable low-growing hedges.

ROCKROSE

Cistus villosus
Biblical term: Myrrh

THE "MYRRH" CONVEYED BY Ishmaelite trading caravans to Egypt in the Joseph story (Genesis 37:25) is usually accepted as the ladanum of commerce. This is a fragrant gum resin exuded by the rockrose, *Cistus villosus*, a species common throughout Palestine, particularly on the dry, rocky ridges and valleys of Mount Carmel. It grows as a small bushy plant, its leaves and stems oozing the soft, dark-brown or black ladanum, which hardens when exposed to air and is collected during the heat of the day. The aromatic gum was prepared extensively by the ancients as an ointment and perfume. Women tucked small bags of the scent in their clothing. Though bitter tasting, the gum was once employed in medicine. Near Dothan, a town on the main trade route between Damascus and Egypt, Joseph was sold by his brothers to camel drivers carrying ladanum in their cargo (Genesis 37:12–36).

The sturdy rockrose is a compact evergreen shrub 3 to 4 feet tall and equally as wide. Its roundish, often wavy-margined leaves of dark green on top, silvery green below, are covered with soft hairs. In late spring it produces purplish-pink flowers with bright yellow centers measuring 2 inches across. For weeks, the plant exhibits an abundance of blossoms. These superb flowers suggest a small, single, brier rose, with five separate petals. A soothing tea is often made from the leaves.

As a native of the Mediterranean region, the rockrose is sun loving and drought resistant. It tolerates poor, dry soil, but prefers a light, moist, well-drained soil with some limestone added. Only in warmer climates does it remain hardy. Elsewhere, treat it as a potted plant to be wintered indoors. Propagation is by seeds sown in spring or from cuttings taken from nonflowering side shoots and rooted in sand.

This beautiful flowering plant is an excellent choice for a sunny slope containing dry, rocky soil or mixed and massed with other biblical plants of similar size and requirements. It looks spectacular in a spacious rock garden. Rockroses can be utilized as informal screens and low dividers, as well as along drives and roadways. Wherever planted the soil must drain quickly and care should be taken not to overwater.

. . . a company of Ishmaelites came from Gilead with their
camels bearing spicery and balm and myrrh.
(Genesis 37:25)

ROSE

Rosa phoenicia
Biblical term: Rose-buds

ALTHOUGH THE NAMES OF SOME plants translated as "roses" in certain versions of the Bible have not been confirmed as roses by botanists, there is little reason to doubt the allusion to "rose-buds" in Wisdom of Solomon 2:8 in the Catholic version of the Bible. At least seven true roses are native to Palestine, the Phoenician rose being the most widely distributed. All of these ancient species are believed to have been introduced from Persia in the course of the centuries. Phoenician roses were cultivated widely in Damascus as the chief source of attar, the fragrant essential oil extracted from the petals for perfumery. Roses were grown in Greece in the fifth century B.C., and they wreathed the heads of Roman revellers. Their sweet odor overwhelmed banquet halls. To early Christians the rose was the emblem of the church, and the five petals symbolized the five wounds of Christ.

Assuming the character of Solomon, the unknown author of Wisdom of Solomon contrasts the after-death rewards of the righteous with those of Jews who seek worldly pleasures and persecute the pious and needy (Wisdom of Solomon 2:8). This literature was written in Greek at Alexandria about 80 B.C. Though excluded from the Protestant Scriptures, it was adopted by early Christians.

The Phoenician rose is a vigorous shrub 3 to 9 feet tall, with long trailing branches armed with hooked prickles. Its oval, coarsely serrated leaflets are glossy, deep green on the upper surface and light green on the lower. Dainty white or pink, single, strongly scented flowers bloom profusely during summer, each bearing five petals and many golden stamens. They look much like the wild roses of the West. In the fall they develop into brilliantly colored oval or round fruits called hips. Oil from the flowers is used in scenting cosmetics, perfumes, and food, but especially for flavoring confections and desserts. Rose hips, rich in vitamin C, are valued for making jelly.

Because the Phoenician rose is little known in this country, you may have to substitute the familiar brier or dog rose, *R. canina,* with single, pale pink blooms, or else a local wild rose. Most roses will grow in any soil not too poor or soggy. For top performance they need a loose, slightly acid soil, plenty of water in dry weather, and feedings in the form of a rose fertilizer. Where summers are hot, afternoon

Let us crown ourselves with rose-buds,
before they be withered.
(Wisdom of Solomon 2:8)

shade is desirable. Annual early springtime pruning is required to remove dead wood, crossing branches, and to keep the plant in bounds.
For seed propagation, the hips must be gathered as soon as ripe and
sown in the spring. Summer cuttings of nearly ripe wood, layering,
and suckers are other means of propagation.

The biblical rose can lend color and beauty to borders, flower beds,
and shrubbery. If preferred, the branches can be trained to climb a
fence, trellis, or wall. Pegged down branches can become a unique
groundcover. Planted in a 14 inch or larger pot the rose will become a
movable ornamental plant.

SAVIN JUNIPER

Juniperus sabina
Biblical term: Heath

THE WORD TRANSLATED "HEATH" in Jeremiah 17:6 is not currently believed to refer to the true heath which does not subsist anywhere in
Palestine and only occasionally in Lebanon and Syria. Though several kinds of juniper grow in Palestine, many authorities take Jeremiah to mean the Savin juniper, *Juniperus sabina*, an evergreen,
shrublike tree commmonly found on barren cliffs and rocky crags in
mountainous regions of Bashan, Galilee and Gilead. Inhabiting the
most desolate and lonely parts of the desert, it manages to survive the
harsh environment. In his message, Jeremiah aptly compares the
man who has turned from God with the solitary juniper. Elsewhere, he
warns the Moabites to flee into the desert and become like the juniper
in order to escape God's wrath (Jeremiah 48:6).

A Savin juniper is much branched, spreading, and shrublike, sometimes attaining a height of 10 to 15 feet, but usually much lower.
Short, sharply pointed, dark green, needlelike leaves stand out from
the twigs on young plants, while scalelike leaves press close to the
slender branches on adult forms. This juniper bears no flowers in the
usual sense. The fully developed fruit is bluish black and fleshy, with
succulent scales fused together to fashion a globular, berrylike structure that takes two years to ripen. Impressed in the glands of the plant
is a poisonous oil once used medicinally. The entire plant emits a
strong, unpleasant odor.

This is among the most beautiful and widely grown of all ever-
greens, being unmatched for its picturesque branches and trunk, for
its hardiness, and its ability to withstand cold with impunity. It is tolerant to drought and unfavorable city conditions. It will grow in dry,
rocky, gravelly ground, but benefits from a moderately moist, limy
soil, and an open, sunny site. Propagation is by seeds which should be
stratified at room temperature 3 to 5 months, by hardwood cuttings
taken in the fall, or by layering.

Continuously covered with decorative foliage, the Savin juniper is
as handsome in winter as in summer. In cold winter climates it is a
perfect subject to serve as a windbreak or screen. There are a number
of lower-growing Savins worth considering for container use or for
rock gardens. For example, variety "Arcadia" is a dense, spreading

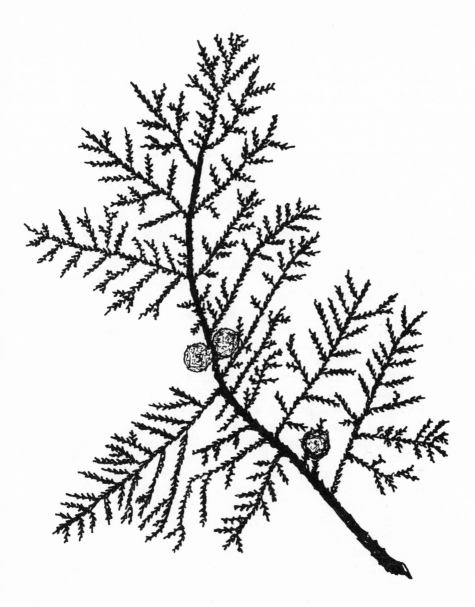

For he shall be like the heath in the desert, and shall not see when good cometh.
    (Jeremiah 17:6)

shrub growing to about 1 ½ feet high and decked with rich green, lacy foliage. Variety *tamariscifolia* grows to about 2 feet and has mostly needlelike foliage. Both varieties adapt readily to bonsai.

SCARLET OAK

Quercus coccifera
Biblical term: Oaks

SCARLET OR KERMES OAK, *Quercus coccifera*, is generously scattered over mountainous areas of Lebanon and Syria and on the dry, hot hillsides of Palestine. On Mount Carmel nine-tenths of the vegetation consists of scarlet oak. Bashan, situated in the highlands to the east of the Sea of Galilee, was famous during the biblical period for its oaks. The prophet Ezekiel, in his forecast against Tyre, likens the impending downfall of the proud and wealthy Phoenician port city to the wreckage of a lavishly equipped seagoing vessel (Ezekiel 27:3–9). Included among the select materials imported to furnish the ship were durable oak timbers from Bashan. These were to be used in making oars for the merchant rowing vessel. A by-product of the oak was the crimson kermes dye extracted from the bodies of small scale insects which feed on the leaves of the tree. They are now replaced by synthetic dyes.

In Bible lands the scarlet oak grows from 6 to 15 feet tall, yet in the United States it can reach 50 to 80 feet. It is an upright shrub or tree of moderate to rapid growth, with a high, open-branching habit and forming a round head. The stiff leaves, dark glossy green above, lighter green beneath, are small and deeply cut, their 7 to 9 lobes tipped with prickly spines. In the fall they turn to a gorgeous scarlet and remain on the tree until spring. Then new leaves appear along with the catkin-borne flowers. The fruits (acorns) ripen during the second year amid the older leaves. Each acorn is set in a spiny cup with spreading scales. Rich in tannins, the bark is used to tan leather and to dye woolens black.

Scarlet oak grows well in fairly dry, deep, rich soil of a light, sandy mixture. It is tolerant of shade, but prefers full sun. When left undisturbed it will eventually grow into a compact evergreen tree. Propagation is easily accomplished by planting acorns in the fall immediately after they have fallen to the ground. Select shiny, plump acorns that have just sprouted, or sprout them yourself between layers of damp peat moss.

The merit of the scarlet oak lies in its high, open-branching habit and beautiful leaves. Its roots grow deep, making it appropriate for lawn or street planting. Producing only moderately dense shade, it is an excellent tree under which to grow smaller biblical plants.

Of the oaks of Bashan have they made thine oars.
(Ezekiel 27:6)

STONE PINE

Pinus pinea
Biblical term: Fir tree

THIS BIBLE PASSAGE (HOSEA 14:8) INDICATES a fruit, most likely of an edible kind. Numerous biblical writers suggest Hosea referred to the stone pine, *Pinus pinea,* which is the only needle-bearing evergreen in his part of the world that produces edible fruits or seeds. The stone pine is one of the most distinctive native trees of southern Europe and the Mediterranean region, renowned for its sweet, nutlike fruits. There the seeds are sold under the names "pinnons" or "Panocchi" and are in much demand to eat either raw or roasted. Since cultivation of the tree dates back into antiquity, it was doubtless well known in Hosea's time. A prophet of the northern kingdom, Hosea saw the threat of Assyrian invasion as a manifestation of God's judgment (Hosea 9:1, 7), because the people of Ephraim (Israel) were immersed in idolatry and Baal worship. In a vision of hope for the nation, Hosea proclaims a new beginning after repentance and purging. He likens a redeemed Israel to the fruitful, evergreen pine tree (Hosea 14:8).

Growing at a moderate rate, the stone pine attains a height of 40 to 80 feet. It is stout, bushy, and round in its youth, later developing a thick, dark, fissured trunk with reddish markings. In middle age it has an umbrellalike crown, which broadens and flattens in old age. Stiff, needlelike leaves of dark to gray green, in pairs, bedeck the numerous branches. The glossy, chestnut-brown, egg-shaped cones, nearly 5 inches long, are covered with thick, hard scales and hide the largest and finest of pine seeds. Oily and rich tasting, they are often used in flavoring confectionery. The wood is used for furniture making and construction work.

Eventually this attractive and valuable pine becomes too overpowering for small gardens. A befitting substitute would be the mugo stone pine, *P. mugo mugus,* a hardy, shrubby, symmetrical little tree, growing slowly to 4 feet in height. It produces dense, dark green needles in pairs, and oval, dark brown cones 1 to 2 inches long. A striking form, it can become an impressive feature in a biblical rock garden. Planted in a container, where it will live for years, it can decorate a doorway or patio. Pruning and shaping turns it into a quick, outstanding bonsai subject.

Both pines will grow in any soil, but a light, well-drained one is best.

. . . I am like a green fir tree. From me is thy fruit found.
(Hosea 14:8)

Once established, they take heat and drought. They are quite hardy everywhere. Propagation is by seeds planted in the spring after all danger from frost has passed.

STORAX

Styrax officinalis
Biblical term: Stacte

A WIDE NUMBER OF WRITERS THINK the "stacte" mentioned in Exodus came from the storax shrub or small tree, *Styrax officinalis,* which grows plentifully on dry hillsides and rocky places in Lebanon, Syria, and throughout Palestine, but primarily around Mount Carmel and Tabor, Gilead and Judea. A resinous gum exudes in drops from this desert plant and more is obtained by making incisions in the branches and stems. The gum has the delicious scent of vanilla, and it is believed the aromatic gum was an ingredient of the holy anointing oil the Lord instructed Moses to prepare for use in the Tabernacle (Exodus 30:34). Gum of the storax and crushed spices were blended, boiled, and united with olive oil to increase the fragrance. This perfumed religious ointment was employed in the anointing of priests such as Aaron and his sons (Exodus 28:41). The gum was also an ingredient in the sacred incense that burned daily in the Tabernacle (30:36).

Unless the lower side branches are clipped, storax grows shrublike 9 to 20 feet or more in height. Deciduous, oval leaves, deep green on top, woolly white beneath, cover the flexible branches. The slender trunk is smooth and gray, its bark being rather sinewy. In June or early July, white, bell-shaped flowers hang in drooping clusters from the ends of the branches, resembling the blooms of lemon and orange trees in appearance and fragrance. These are followed by fleshy, green, hairy, and roundish fruits which, when dried, are used to make rosaries.

With its graceful foliage and the pleasant aroma of the flowers, the *officinalis* species is an ideal contribution to the biblical garden. However, it is not hardy where winters are severe. The equally attractive fragrant snowbell, *S. obassia,* is completely hardy and could act as a substitute. Between May and June it produces drooping clusters of white, bell-like flowers at the ends of its branches. The height of both species is about the same.

Either storax does well in open sunlight or part shade, and in a good, porous garden soil irrigated with generous applications of water. Pruning the lower branches not only keeps the plant treelike, but also displays the handsome trunk and bark. Propagation is by seeds sown soon after ripening or by layering.

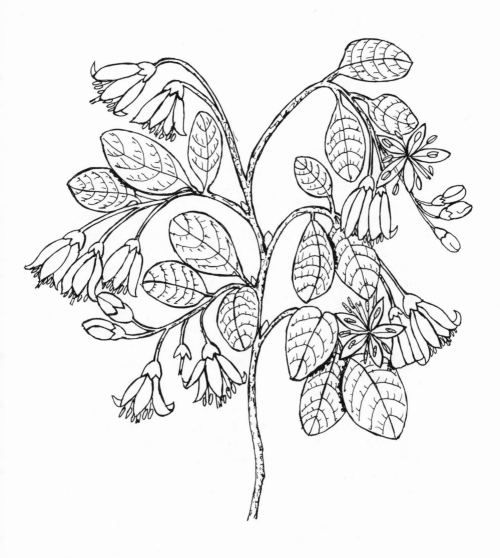

And the Lord said unto Moses, Take unto thee sweet spices, stacte, and onycha, and galbanum.
(Exodus 30:34)

Storax is attractive against a background of evergreen trees or as a specimen on a lawn. Since the roots are not aggressive, it is a fine tree under which to plant biblical flowers.

SYCOMORE FIG

Ficus sycomorus
Biblical term: Sycomore tree

THE SYCOMORE TREE OF THE BIBLE is native to Egypt and Syria, but has been cultivated for centuries on low hills and mountainous regions of Palestine. Often the trees were planted along roadsides and caravan routes to afford shade to travelers. This is a vigorous growing tree, 30 to 40 feet tall, with a short, thick trunk that usually divides into wide-spreading, gnarled, and twisted branches, the lower ones nearly sweeping the ground. It was an easy tree for a small man like the tax collector Zacchaeus to climb and catch a view of Jesus as he entered the city of Jericho. (Luke 19:1–4). The prophet Amos, whose home was in the mountain-top village of Tekoa (Amos 1:1), called himself a "dresser of sycomore trees" (7:14), referring to his occupation of pricking holes in the figlike fruit with a sharp tool to speed up ripening.

A tree topped with a huge, round-headed crown and dense ever-green foliage, the sycomore fig may attain a trunk 20 or more feet in girth. Its fragrant, somewhat heart-shaped leaves are smooth above, slightly hairy beneath. The inch-long, yellowish, black-spotted fruit is produced in abundance several times a year on the twigs and stems of the branches and trunk. Though the fruit is much inferior in size and taste to that of the common fig, it did, and still does, furnish food for the poor of the Near East. The wood of this long-lived tree is soft and porous, yet durable enough for constructing furniture. Mummy cases built of sycomore wood three thousand years ago remain in excellent condition.

As with the common fig, the sycomore tree requires protection in extremely cold winter climates. When a hard freeze occurs, the wood freezes back, but recovers after the weather warms. It will grow in sun or shade in any soil and once established is drought resistant. Lower limbs that interfere with one's walking beneath the tree should be pruned. Propagation is by cuttings that root readily.

The effect of a sycomore fig when bearing fruit is a picture not soon forgotten. Its attractiveness is prolonged by nearly year-around foliage, going bare only for a short time in midyear while new leaves are forming. As an ornamental and shade tree it is unmatched. Birds are drawn to the fruit and find protection in the branches.

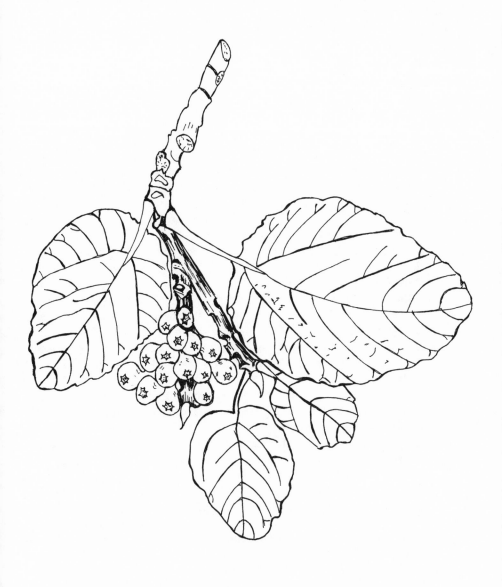

*And he ran before, and climbed up into a sycomore tree to see
him: for he was to pass that way.*
(Luke 19:4)

TAMARISK

Tamarix aphylla
Biblical term: Grove

THE "GROVE" OF THE GENESIS passage has been identified as tamarisk, a large shrub or small tree found in arid, desert regions, even growing naturally in pure sand. Tamarisk is native to Egypt and Syria, with approximately eight species inhabiting Palestine. The town of Beersheba, located on the fringe of the desert, was a favorite place for the nomadic patriarch Abraham to pitch his tents (Isaiah 54:2), for the numerous wells kept his flocks and herds supplied with water. After reaching an agreement with Abimelech, the local ruler, in regard to a well (Genesis 21:22–32), Abraham planted a tamarisk tree "and called there on the name of the Lord" (21:33). Abraham was adhering to the Canaanite custom of planting a tree in commemoration of a special occasion. Later Saul, the first king of Israel, met with his counselors under a tamarisk tree (I Samuel 22:6). His bones and those of his three sons were buried beneath a tamarisk at Jabesh (I Samuel 31:8–13).

There is a lacy beauty and charm about the tamarisk, which ultimately reaches 20 to 30 feet in height. Though the trunk has a sturdy and cedarlike appearance, the branches are extremely slender, and tiny scalelike leaves of silvery blue-green completely clothe the jointed twigs. This gives the foliage an evergreen, juniperlike aspect. A sharp contrast becomes apparent when the airy, minute, white to pinkish flowers open in clusters at the ends of the branches in late summer. The blossoms bestow a brightness to the habitually drab state of the southern Negeb where Abraham wandered. In time, his memorial tree would furnish shade for other travelers and a sheltered retreat in which to worship.

The species of tamarisk described is particularly suited to dry, alkaline conditions. A species adaptable to most of our climates, and with a close resemblance to the tamarisk, is the salt cedar, *T. pentandra,* a feathery shrub 10 to 15 feet high. It has pale, blue-green, juniperlike foliage and bears dense clusters of tiny pale pink flowers in midsummer. Sharp pruning each spring curtails the shrub's tendency toward lankiness.

All tamarisks have resistance to wind and drought, a tolerance for salt, and the ability to conform to almost any soil. Exposure to sun or

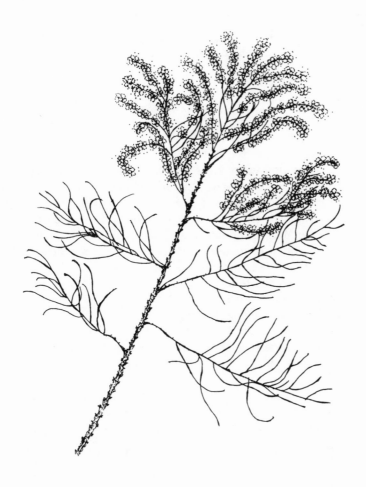

*And Abraham planted a grove in Beer-sheba, and called there
on the name of the Lord.*
   (Genesis 21:33)

semishade is important to their culture. When heavily damaged by
below-zero temperatures, they rapidly restore themselves. Tamarisks may be propagated by seeds, but cuttings of ripened wood root
easily in sand or in well-watered open ground. They should be cut
back to 12 to 15 inches when transplanted.

   Deep tap roots make tamarisks difficult to maintain in containers
for a long period of time. In a biblical garden they are best used as a
rich-looking hedge or as dense background plants. The flowers and
foliage are delightful for bouquets.

TEREBINTH

Pistacia terebinthus
Biblical term: Teil

MODERN AUTHORITIES AGREE THAT THE "teil tree" of the Isaiah passage is erroneously translated in the King James Version. It has been identified as the terebinth, *Pistacia terebinthus,* a small deciduous tree found in stony soil on the dry lower slopes of hills in Palestine, as well as in the entire Mediterranean region. In a vision the prophet Isaiah saw the nation of Israel invaded again and again, its people killed or exiled by enemies. He compares the coming days (Isaiah 6:11–12) to a terebinth and an oak felled by woodcutters, who discard the limbs on the ground. But, he promises, just as the stump of a tree regains its strength and in time grows new limbs, so shall Israel survive. Isaiah then points out that even though a tree is bare of foliage in winter, it sprouts fresh leaves in spring. Thus, in the same way shall the tiny remnant left of Israel once more flourish under the dominion of God (Isaiah 6:13).

In its leafless state, the terebinth resembles the deciduous Tabor oak, *Quercus ithaburensis,* mentioned by Isaiah, but the terebinth grows in places too warm for the oak. A sturdy, shapely tree with purplish-gray bark, it reaches 20 to 25 feet in height. Compound leaves of a reddish hue unfold on the branches in spring. Wee greenish- or reddish-purple flowers bloom in dense clusters at the same time as the young leaves appear. They are followed by branched clusters of small, round coral-red fruits, which later turn brown. When the bark and outer wood is chipped, a transparent, yellowish fluid flows out, releasing a strong resinous odor. On exposure to air, the fluid becomes dry, thick, and brittle. Known as Chian, Scio, or Cypress turpentine, the sweet-tasting gum has been used internally and externally as a drug since at least as early as the time of Hippocrates. Some authorities suggest the "spicery" carried from Palestine to Egypt (Genesis 43:11) came from the terebinth tree. An oil is extracted from the fruits, and the dark, hard wood is used in cabinet making.

Unfortunately this exceptionally fine biblical tree is almost nonexistent in the United States. Less difficult to acquire, yet equal in desirability, is the Chinese pistache, *P. chinensis,* growing moderately to 60 feet tall. It is a broadly rounded tree with a short trunk and com-

94

But yet in it shall be a tenth, and it shall return, and shall be eaten: as a teil tree, and as an oak.
(Isaiah 6:13)

pound deciduous leaves that turn a vivid orange-red in the fall. The female tree bears brilliant red fruits that later change to dark blue. The tree is entirely hardy as far north as Philadelphia.

Closely allied to the pistachio nut tree, the Chinese pistache has identical cultural requirements (see Pistachio). Either the terebinth or the Chinese pistache tree would add beauty to a landscape scene positioned in a corner of a small biblical garden. They are spectacular when established as single specimens on a lawn or to shade a patio.

WALNUT

Juglans regia
Biblical term: Nuts

IN SONG OF SOLOMON 6:11, THE GROOM-TO-BE of the lovely Shulamite maiden speaks of passing through a garden of "nuts," apparently referring to King Solomon's extensive garden a few miles from Jerusalem. Today the majority of biblical scholars concur that the writer of the poetic verse meant the fruit of the tree *Juglans regia,* commonly called English or Persian walnut. The place of origin of the walnut was Persia, not England, and it was introduced into Palestine as long ago as the time of Solomon. Now the tree grows everywhere in the higher elevations of Palestine, scattered about in woods, near streams, and by village wells. Since the kernels of the nuts are a source of flavorful and nourishing food, and since the trees offer cool dense shade in summer, Solomon must have received a great amount of pleasure from his walnut orchard. The luxury of fruit-bearing trees could be afforded only by kings and rich men (Ecclesiates 2:4–6).

Providing both utility and beauty, and often living for centuries, the English walnut quickly attains a height up to 60 feet, with a proportionate spread of the crown. Bark of the long, straight, massive trunk is silvery gray and smooth when young, but becomes deeply fissured with age. The bark is used for tanning leather. The aromatic, deciduous, lustrous leaves are typically divided into 5 to 7 leaflets, each 3 to 6 inches long. Small, greenish flowers, hanging in slender catkins, antecede the fleshy, oval, green husks that encase the wrinkled nutshells. Within the shells lie the oily seeds, or nuts. A source of nourishing food, they are eaten raw or in cookery. A brown dye is obtained from the husks, and the dark-colored timber is treasured for furniture making. The wood is also valued for veneers and gun stocks, as it takes a beautiful polish. Formerly the leaves were used in medicine.

The principal climatic hazard for the English walnut is injury from early frost and severe cold. Better adapted to most parts of the United States is the eastern European Carpathian mountain strain of walnut. It looks like the English walnut, but is much hardier and survives temperatures of -30 degrees F. Fast growing, it soon reaches a height of 30 to 40 feet. In the fall it yields quantities of high-quality nuts. Plant two near each other for good pollination.

Walnut trees favor a fertile, well-drained soil and plenty of sun-

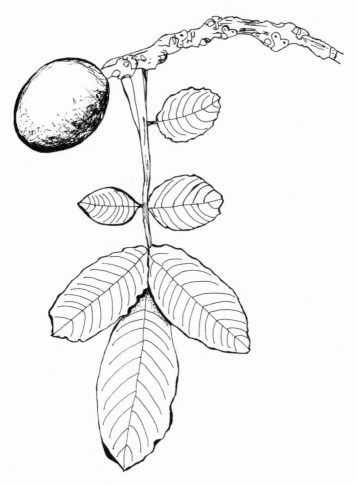

I went down into the garden of nuts
to see the fruits of the valley.
  (Song of Solomon 6:11)

shine. Established plants can stand some drought, but to produce choice nuts they need deep, regular waterings in regions where summers are dry. Propagation is by seed which should be stratified and planted directly after the nuts ripen in October and November. Transplant young seedlings in the spring.

An attractive tree for shade, with a bonus of delectable nuts, the walnut tree is a rewarding plant to add to a biblical orchard. It usually begins to bear nuts four to seven years after planting. Feeder roots grow within the drip line, so do not plant flowers beneath the branches.

WHITE POPLAR

Populus alba
Biblical term: Poplars

NATIVES OF PALESTINE, WHITE POPLARS grow wild in moist wooded low-lands, by springs, or along watercourses. They have long been culti-vated for shade because of their adaptability, fast growth, and thick foliage. After the Hebrews entered Canaan they frequently adopted the Canaanite practice of worshiping Baal images. They conducted the cultic rites beneath poplars and other trees considered sacred (Hosea 4:13). Often the trees were planted in groves on high eleva-tions (II Kings 17:10). Altars under the trees were for receiving sacrifi-cial offerings and for burning incense dedicated to the worship of the large number of Baals (II Chronicles 33:3). For generations the prophets of God denounced the groves concealing the activities of these agricultural fertility cults. Hosea in his message to the northern kingdom (Israel) graphically descibes the corruptions brought about by idolatry (Hosea 4:1-19).

The beautiful white poplar rapidly reaches 40 to 60 feet in height, with a rounded spreading head and curving branches. Both branches and trunk are covered by a smooth, grayish bark, but the annual shoots are very white when young. The deciduous 3 to 5 lobed leaves, lustrous bright green above, snowy white and woolly beneath, create a pleasing sight as they spin in the slightest air movement. At the end of March tiny crimson male and greenish-yellow female flowers ap-pear in dangling catkins. The seed capsules burst open in May to shed the ripened seeds. Coating the young buds and twigs is a resinous var-nish which sends forth a sweet aromatic odor in spring. Logs of large white poplars produce a soft, white, light wood used for pulp and to construct crates, packing boxes, and toys.

Though the white poplar is attractive and splendid for shade, its faults are short life, brittle branches, persistent suckers requiring re-moval, and invasive roots running close to the surface of the soil. To offset these features, the tree gives a quick effect, thrives in the poor-est soils, and withstands climatic conditions which few other trees will tolerate, including extreme cold and desert heat. Propagation is by seeds, suckers, and hardwood cuttings taken in the fall.

If you have plenty of space, the biblical white poplar will perform well as a tall border along a driveway or as a sentinel by a gate. Rows of them are commonly planted for windbreaks, property dividers, and to abate soil erosion.

*They sacrifice upon the tops of the mountains, and burn
incense upon the hills, under oaks and poplars and elms,
because the shadow thereof is good.*

(Hosea 4:13)

WHITE WILLOW

Salix alba
Biblical term: Willow tree

ROUGHLY TWENTY-ONE KINDS OF TRUE willows are native to Palestine, all found lining the banks of brooks and rivers or wherever else the roots can draw a year-round supply of moisture. One of the most plentiful in Palestine is the white willow, *Salix alba*, a small graceful tree rarely reaching the height it does in eastern North America, where it is often an escapee from cultivation. The pliable branches and tender twigs make this willow a fit subject for Ezekiel to employ in his parable of the two eagles, in which he addresses his people prior to the destruction of Jerusalem.

In the symbolic prophecy (Ezekiel 17:5), he portrays Zedekiah (a descendant of David), made king of Judah by Nebuchadnezzar (a powerful eagle), as "the seed of the land," likening him to a willow planted beside "great waters" (Palestine). But after awhile the willow bends toward the second eagle, the ruler of Egypt. By doing so, he deceives the first eagle. The substance of the message is that because Zedekiah violates his pledge of loyalty, he will be brought to Babylon and punished for his treachery (15–20). Within five years Ezekiel's forecast materialized (II Kings 25:6, 7).

Rapid growing but short lived, the white willow at maturity is estimated to be from 40 to 60 feet in height, with even a greater spread. It has a short, thick trunk with slender upright branches. In winter the bare golden yellow branches and twigs glow with color. Their greatest beauty lies in the deciduous, long, and pointed leaves attached to the twigs. These are coated with silvery hairs and give a frosty sheen to the foliage. As the young leaves begin to expand, flowers encased in catkins become visible. Tufts of hairs at the base of the ripened fruits help in scattering the seeds. The pliant young twigs are often woven into baskets, and the light, firm wood furnishes material for flooring.

There are several dwarf willows suitable for low hedges or container gardening. Perhaps the best is the Arctic willow *S. pururea* "Nana," a compact shrub growing to 3 feet, with lovely gray-green foliage. It can be clipped and held to 12 inches in height and 12 inches in width or left to grow naturally.

Both tree and dwarf forms withstand the coldest of temperatures, take any kind of soil, tolerate poor drainage, but do grow best under

He took also the seed of the land, and planted it in a fruitful field; he placed it by great waters, and set it as a willow tree.

(Ezekiel 17:5)

average garden conditions. They require an ample supply of water and a position in full sun or light shade. Propagation is by seeds sown as the capsules open or by cuttings which root easily in most soil.

For the biblical garden, the white willow tree is effective as a shrub background or as a screen for blocking out undesirable views and buildings. It is especially valuable for erosion control on stream and river banks.

PART 2

Everyday Food Plants

The basic food in Bible lands was and still is bread (Isaiah 3:1), with the production of cereal grains a major part of life. Israelite farmers, emulating the agricultural methods practiced by the Canaanites, sowed the seed in small fields (Leviticus 27:16), which were usually handed down from their ancestors. Stone walls or hedges surrounded the fields for protection against animals and humans. Drought and crop failure were constant dangers, for yields depended almost entirely upon the distribution of rainfall in the fall and winter seasons (Deuteronomy 11:10–11). To round out the diet, pulse and other vegetable crops were planted in fenced plots of ground. Ezekiel, in his foreboding discourse before the fall of Jerusalem, implies a coming severe shortage of bread by listing a wide mixture of ingredients used in making bread (Ezekiel 4:9). Enemies would prevent food from entering the city, thus causing a famine.

Making bread from the crops named by Ezekiel was a daily task of Palestinian womenfolk. After grinding the seeds into meal by mortar and pestle or between two flat stones, it was mixed with salt and water to form a dough. Leaven in Old Testament times consisted of a piece of fermented dough saved from an earlier making. It was mixed into the fresh dough in a trough, shaped into thin loaves, and might be baked in the oven of a public baker (Hosea 7:4). Unleavened dough was used in the celebration of the Feast of the Unleavened Bread (Exodus 12:15, 13:6–8) and for the Passover anniversary (Numbers 28: 16–17).

Ezekiel 4:9 contains almost a complete register of the grain and pulse crops referred to in the Bible: wheat, barley, beans lentils, millet, and fitches. A rewarding experience would be to

reserve a section of your biblical garden for a sampling of each of the plants. An alternative is to grow the plants indoors, housing them in pots, bowls, or shallow dishes. Though the seeds planted in containers produce smaller specimens, the emergence of the soft tender growth and consequential development will trigger the same thoughts about the crops of such vital importance in biblical times.

The grains, when dried, make excellent backgrounds to flower arrangements. They can be preserved by hanging them upside down in a dry, airy place until they are dry and crisp.

WHEAT

Triticum satiuum
Biblical term: Wheat

WHEAT AS THE SOURCE OF BREADSTUFFS was and still is the most commanding cereal grass in the world. Cultivated since antiquity, it was first recorded in Genesis 30:14. It was preferred above barley and sold for triple the price (II Kings 7:1). The best of each new crop was dedicated to God (Numbers 18:12). During Solomon's reign wheat had become such an important commodity in Palestine that the king included it in his payments to Hiram of Tyre (II Chronicles 2:10). Wheat retained its position in New Testament days and formed the foundation of many of Jesus' parables (Matthew 13:25; Mark 4: 29; John 12:24). The word "corn" mentioned in the parables and elsewhere in the Bible covers various grains. Our corn, or maize, was unknown until the discovery of the New World. Wheat grains roasted or boiled remain a favorite food in Palestine. Much of the grain is ground into flour and baked into flat cakes of bread. For the poor of the Near East, wheat bread is an unattainable luxury.

In ancient Palestine plowing of the fields took place as soon as the first rains softened the soil, usually in mid-October. Directly thereafter the wheat seed was broadcast by hand and then ploughed in or trodden upon by cattle (Isaiah 32:20). Harvesting of the wheat started about four months after plowing. Following the threshing (II Samuel 24:21–22; I Chronicles 21:20–23) and the winnowing (Isaiah 41:15–16) came a time of great rejoicing and feasting (Deuteronomy 16:9–15). The "Feast of Weeks" marked the end of the wheat harvest (Exodus 34:22).

The wheat plant itself grows from 4 to 5 feet high. It is an annual grass with long, narrow, flat leaf blades fitted around each joint of a normally hollow stem. The minute flowers, borne on tiny branchlets, crowd together on terminal spikes. After wind pollination, the flowers develop into seeds (wheat grains), which ripen within thirty days or less, depending upon the area. Commonly cultivated in Palestine are bearded kinds of wheat that have prickly hairs in the husks of the kernels.

Wheat is best adapted to loam or clay soils well supplemented with organic material and located in the temperate, drier regions of the world. Propagation is by seed placed in moist soil at 65 degrees F. Germination occurs in three or four days.

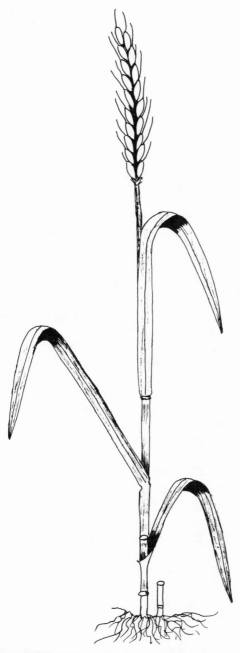

Take thou also unto thee wheat, and barley, and beans, and lentiles, and millet, and fitches, and put them in one vessel, and make thee bread.
(Ezekiel 4:9)

BARLEY

Hordeum hexastichon
Biblical term: Barley

BARLEY WAS CULTIVATED IN THE Near East long before wheat, and in Bible lands barley is the most widely distributed of all cereal crops. The popularity of barley lies in its ability to withstand poorer soils, heat, and drought better than any other grain. Moreover, it requires a shorter period to ripen (Exodus 9:31). In ancient Palestine, barley was, and even is today, a leading food used to fatten livestock. Because wheat was extremely expensive, poor villagers used barley by itself or mixed with other crops to make a coarse and heavy bread (Ezekiel 4:9). Hence barley became the symbol of poverty and was held in low esteem by the wealthy.

Winter barley, *Hordeum hexastichon*, was sown in Palestine between the end of October and the middle of November, with the harvesting taking place in time for the Passover (Joshua 5:11). Harvesting was a joyful, happy occasion (Isaiah 9:3), when entire families worked in the fields for about seven weeks. Grain left in the fields was gleaned by widows, orphans, the poor, or sojourners (Ruth 2). According to Hebrew law, the owner of the field could not clear the corners nor the grain that had fallen loose on the ground (Leviticus 19:9; 23:22; Deuteronomy 24:19).

At least two other species of barley were cultivated in ancient Palestine. One was spring barley, *H. vulgare,* which was sown after winter had passed and harvested in summer. It could be grown in northern Palestine where summers are too short to ripen wheat.

Barley grows from 1 to 4 feet tall, depending upon the variety. An annual grass with light green leaves, it is similar in structure to wheat. The main difference between the two grains takes place in the seedheads. Barley can usually be recognized by the long, bristlelike attachments on the dense flowering clusters. The seeds (kernels) are shuttle-shaped, grooved, and husked. Embodied in them are enzymes and protein of high nutritional value.

Today there is a type of barley ideally suited to every climate in the world. Even though it will grow where other grains fail to thrive, far better crops are produced on good soil and in moderate temperatures. Barley is largely grown in Western lands for the transformation of kernels into malt, the material from which ale, beer, and stout are prepared. Some of the grain is in demand as livestock feed. A smaller amount is hulled for human consumption.

There is a lad here, which hath five barley loaves, and two small fishes: but what are they among so many?
(John 6:9)

BEANS

Vicia faba
Biblical term: Beans

FROM EARLIEST TIMES THE HORSE, *faba,* or broad bean has been widely cultivated in Egypt, Palestine, and Syria as a source of food. The dry seeds were ground, even as now, into a coarse meal for bread making (Ezekiel 4:9) by the poorer people living in biblical lands. Green, immature pods are boiled whole in salted water and eaten as a vegetable, while ripe green beans are often added to stews or cooked with onions, olive oil, and a fragment of meat. When David was fleeing Jerusalem during Absalom's rebellion, broad beans were included among the provisions contributed by his friends (II Samuel 17:27–29).

Having originated in the Mediterranean region, broad bean is the principal bean of Europe. It is a hardy, leguminous annual, growing upright in bush-form to 5 feet or more in height. The ovalish leaves are divided into two to six pairs of medium-green leaflets. Small, white, sweet-pea-like flowers bloom from the bottom upward on a single main stalk, each marked by a purplish-black spot on the two side petals. When in blossom, the flowers issue a sweet scent. The thick, glossy, green pods, from 7 to 12 inches long, are borne in the axils of the leaves. Each contains five to seven large, oblong, flattened, light green seeds (beans), which turn brown or black upon drying.

In Palestine the seeds are planted after the first rains of fall, and if they are to be used as dry beans they are usually harvested in the spring. By then the pods have reached mature size and the plants are quite withered, whereupon the bean crop is beaten out with sticks or flails. As with wheat and barley, the crop in the past was stored underground in pits, with the openings covered, or else in pottery jars. Rich in protein, broad beans provide a food of great nutritional value.

The broad bean will not tolerate hot weather and is grown only during winter in the warmer parts of the temperate zones; but in cooler regions it is grown in the summer. Heavy yielding and hardier than other beans, it can be used as a substitute for lima beans where the growing season is short. Due to the broad bean's slow growth, seeds should be sown as early in the season as possible. Broad beans are drought resistant and take poor soils, but produce better under more favorable conditions. Like any legume they add nitrogen to the soil.

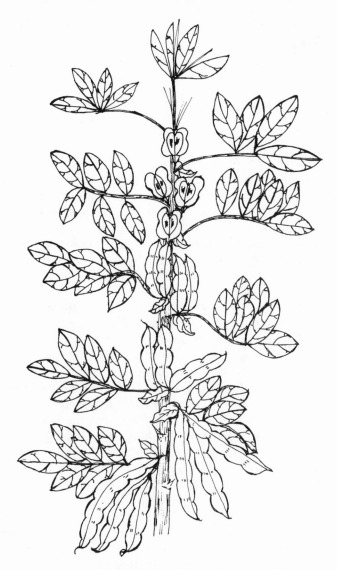

*Brought . . . beans . . . for David and for the
people that were with him, to eat.*
(II Samuel 17:28–29)

When shredded the dry plants make a beneficial mulch or compost
material.

Some people have a genetic trait which causes a severe allergic or
even toxic reaction to broad beans. Very few have such a response,
but it is advisable to sample small amounts of the beans before eating
them in large portions.

LENTIL

Lens esculenta (Ervum lens)
Biblical term: Lentiles

WILD LENTIL IS A SMALL, LEGUMINOUS annual which has long been cultivated in Egypt, Palestine, and Syria as well as in other lands of the
Near East for the yield of its nourishing seeds (II Samuel 23:11). Lentils were included along with beans and other supplies for David and
his men (17:27–28), and in times of scarcity the seeds were made into
bread (Ezekiel 4:9). For the poor living in those countries, lentil bread
with a little barley added was and still is a major food. Parched seeds
are commonly eaten, too.

There are a number of varieties of lentils cultivated in Bible lands,
differing in height, color of leaves, flowers and seeds. It is believed the
red pottage of lentils for which Esau sold his birthright (Genesis
25:29–34) was made from the red Egyptian variety so widely grown in
Eastern countries. The thick soup (or stew) prepared from lentils and
herbs (II Kings 4:39) is boiled with or without meat and affects a reddish color. In eating this savory dish, Esau would double his flat,
round bread spoon-fashion and dip it into the bowl. Containing a
wealth of protein, pottage comprises a satisfying and wholesome
meal.

The lentil plant varies from 6 to 18 inches in height, producing
many, long, hairy ascending branches. Its compound leaves, consisting of five to seven pairs of oblong leaflets, terminate in tendrils. One
to three small pea-blossom-like, white flowers striped with violet
form on a long axillary stalk. Each short, broadly oblong pod that develops from the flowers holds two lens-shaped seeds about the size of
a small pea, alternating in color from yellow or ash-gray to dark
brown, but sometimes mottled or speckled. Due to its superior flavor
and small seeds, the reddish variety is the most highly regarded in the
Near East. The green plant is valued as fodder for livestock.

In Palestine lentil seed is sown after the rains start in the fall. It is
often raised on poor, dry soil unsuited for other crops. The seeds in
Bible times were beaten out with a staff. In the United States the dry
seeds find use for gravies, salads, soups, and main dishes, while the
green plant enriches the soil and provides fodder for cattle, hogs, and
sheep. The culture is the same as for the broad bean (see Beans).

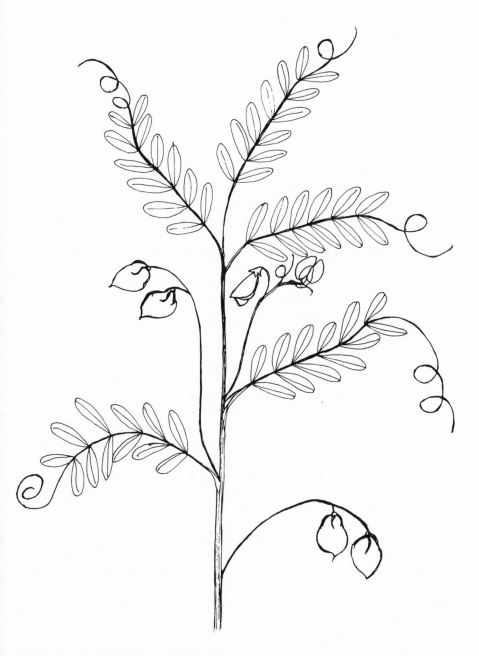

And the Philistines were gathered together into a troop, where was a piece of ground full of lentiles.
(II Samuel 23:11)

MILLET

Panicum miliaceum
Biblical term: Millet

COMMON MILLET, ALSO CALLED BROOM-CORN and Indian millet, is one of the first grains domesticated by man. A cereal crop, it has been cultivated in Egypt and Palestine since earliest times for human consumption as well as for feeding livestock. The tiny seeds, smallest of all grains, are used to decorate cakes, but also are eaten raw or cooked as the greater part of the everyday diet for millions who live in Eastern lands. As in ancient days, the seeds are a component of pottage or are ground into a meal to prepare coarse, flat, unleavened bread. Upon heating a few minutes, the bread develops a crisp crust. Sometimes millet meal was combined with other grains and legumes for bread-making (Ezekiel 4:9).

Millet seed was broadcast in Palestinian fields in early spring, with the plants receiving little or no cultivation during the hot, dry growing season. The crop had to be harvested as soon as the seed clusters dried, for the seeds fall out soon upon ripening. After cutting with sickles, the crop was carried to the threshing floor where women trod upon the seed heads. Afternoon breezes blew away the husks.

The robust annual grass grows upright from 2 to 4 feet high. It possesses many-branched, slender stalks bearing soft, broad, flat leaves about 10 inches in length. The foot-long flowering head are plump, clustered, and drooping. Each ripened cluster contains a multitude of hard, round seeds. Inside the smooth, shiny, white seed coat are rich layers of gluten-free, nutritious food.

Although millet tolerates dry and poor soil, best results are achieved by keeping the soil moist and by using a good garden loam. Required is a site in full sun and the seeds sown in rows. When the seedlings reach 3 inches in height, they should be thinned to 4 to 6 inches apart. Like numerous other grasses, millet forms many-stemmed clumps as it matures. Fully developed seed heads dry into tawny, orangey shades, making them attractive subjects for long-lasting arrangements.

In the United States millet is grown commercially for hay, and the dried, stiff heads are bound together for brooms. The seeds are sold to feed birds, poultry, and livestock. A growing number of people serve the healthful grain as a breakfast cereal or use it as a substitute for rice in casseroles, meat loaves, soups, and vegetarian dishes.

Judah, and the land of Israel, they were thy merchant; they traded in thy market wheat of Minnith, and Pannag (millet), and honey, and oil, and balm.
(Ezekiel 27:17)

SPELT

Triticum aestivum var. *spelta*
Biblical term: Fitches and Rie

MANY SCHOLARS CONSIDER THE WORD translated from Hebrew as "fitches" in Ezekiel 4:9 (page 105) as meaning spelt, an inferior variety of wheat cultivated in Egypt for thousands of years but thought to have originated in Mesopotamia. In Babylonia, a beer was brewed from barley and spelt, and used for sacrificial purposes. Although spelt is not present in Palestine today, it is believed to have been a staple grain crop in biblical times.

The "rie" that escaped the plague of hail visited on Egypt because of the stubbornness of the pharoah (Exodus 9:32), and the "rie" planted as a border around more profitable fields of wheat and barley (Isaiah 28:25) have been identified as spelt. True rye, *secale cereale*, was unknown in Egypt, Palestine, and Syria in biblical times. It is a cereal crop suited to colder and more northernly regions of the world. Not until the Middle Ages did rye become widely distributed in the cooler parts of Europe.

Spelt is an annual grass growing to about 3 feet high, distinguished from common wheat by a shorter, stouter stem and stiffer spikes of grain. Its dense, slender, loose spikes are usually without long beards, and the ends of the hard, triangular kernels have no hairs. Since the grains are held tightly in the shafts, threshing does not remove the hulls. In Europe spelt is an important grain crop, produced in great quantities for consumption by humans, but also valued as a food for livestock. It is grown in the United States to a more limited extent for the same purposes.

The chief advantage of spelt is its ability to grow on poor soils and to yield a sizable crop on land unadaptable for other cereals, especially common wheat. Hearty and nutritious, spelt bread was regarded in biblical times as superior to that made of barley.

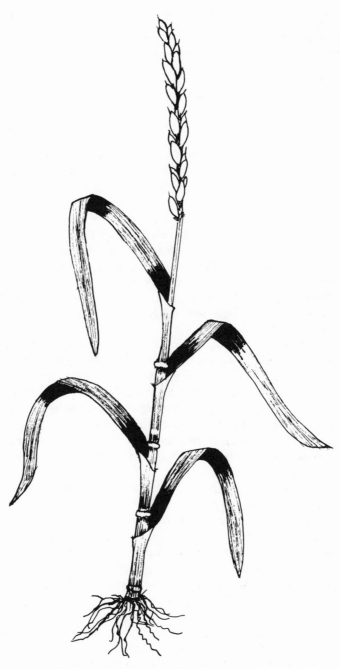

But the wheat and the rie were not smitten:
for they were not grown up.
(Exodus 9:32)

DURRA

Holcus sorghum var. *durra*
Biblical term: Reed

THERE HAVE BEEN TREMENDOUS differences of opinion in respect to the word "reed" cited in Mark 15:36 and in Matthew 27:48. Today many authorities grant that the reed upon which the vinegar-soaked sponge was placed to lift to the lips of Jesus refers to the sorghum commonly called durra. It is a medium- to stout-stemmed cereal grass, reaching a height of 6 feet in the Nile Delta and Palestine. The "hyssop" mentioned in John 19:29 may also refer to this same type of sorghum. Seeds produced on the huge flowering heads of the plant are ground into a nutty-tasting meal for making porridge and a coarse, flat bread. Because the seeds are often roasted and eaten out of hand, some writers suggest durra was the "parched corn" given to Ruth by Boaz (Ruth 2:14).

A native of tropical Africa, durra was carried to other parts of the world and for centuries has been cultivated in biblical lands, primarily as a grain crop for humans, the stalks and leaves being fed to livestock. Under favorable conditions, this robust annual grows to 15 feet high. Leaves on the stiff, pithy stalks resemble field corn, but are only about one third the size. Both leaves and stalks have a white, waxy coating. The large, terminal flowering clusters develop into numerous shining seeds, ovalish in shape, and somewhat smaller than grains of wheat.

Over the years hundreds of different strains of durra have evolved. The flowers vary in color from yellowish to orange or red, the seeds from pearly white to yellow, red, or brown. Seeds may or may not stay in the hulls after threshing. The pith may be juicy or dry, sweet or tasteless, depending upon the strain. In the United States durra is an important cereal crop, cultivated chiefly as a dry grain for animal food, but sometimes as forage or silage. The grain is also used in making dextrose, paste, starch, and alcoholic drinks.

Quick growing durra is best adapted to warm climates, where summers are long and hot. It is extremely resistant to drought, even performing well on sandy soils in desert areas without irrigation. However, yields vastly improve with irrigation and in the richer loams of ordinary garden soil. Growing conditions are like that of field corn. The seeds of this frost-sensitive plant should be sown in a sunny location when the weather has thoroughly settled.

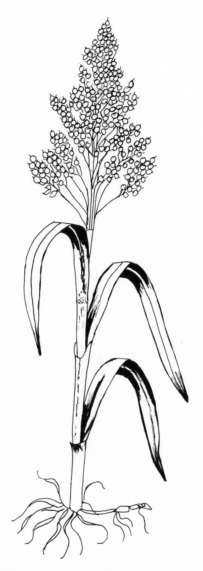

*And one ran and filled a sponge full of vinegar, and put it on a
reed, and gave him to drink.*
(Mark 15:36)

In the biblical garden, durra can be grouped with the grains already
noted. Its handsome foliage and colorful flowering head and seeds
have all the desirable qualities for a thick ornamental hedge or
screen. Seeds of durra attract birds to the garden. The tops of the
stalks are useful for flower arrangements.

SUGAR CANE

Saccharum officinarum
Biblical term: Sweet cane

THE "SWEET CANE" MENTIONED in Isaiah 43:24 is now generally regarded as the true sugar cane, *Saccharum officinarum*. The origin of
this principal carbohydrate food plant is unknown. Before recorded
history it was cultivated in semitropical and tropical regions of the
world. Jeremiah 6:20 refers to a "good cane from a far country." It
was probably carried by Arab traders from India to Tyre, making the
cane an expensive import. The Hebrews, not knowing how to refine
sugar, used the sweet juicy sap in the stalks for sweetening food, beverages, and as a confection. Presently, sugar cane is grown extensively in Israel.

During the exile in Babylon the Second Isaiah, through messages
from God, comforts his fellow captives with promises of deliverance.
The prophet in verse 43:24 reproaches them for lack of confidence in
their God. Making a play on the words, "bought me no sugar cane,"
he points out their half-hearted approach to worship services.

From this giant grass comes most of the world's sugar. The solid
jointed stalks, attaining a height of 10 to 20 feet, are filled with soft,
long fibers. They may be a pale green, reddish purple, or conspicu-
ously striped white and green. The leaves are cornlike, gracefully
arching, with rough or cutting edges. At maturity the stalk is sur-
mounted by a fluffy, plumelike tassel containing hundreds of tiny
flowers. These beautifully colored flowers vary from a soft lavender to
a dark purple, depending upon the variety. The canes yield a dark
brown, slightly acid juice that is 10 to 12 percent sugar. In less ad-
vanced countries the cane is still cut by hand, the juice being boiled
until it can be deposited into wooden molds to form flat, sticky cakes.

Hundreds of varieties of sugar cane are cultivated today. All of
them are hybrids developed by plant breeders. The cane grows best in
strong sunlight, where climates are damp from frequent rainfall, or
where abundant water is available by irrigation. Soil must be rich or
have richness added to it. Commercial cane-growing in the United
States is limited to Hawaii and the southern states. Propagation is almost entirely from pieces of stalks, and the cane is harvested by ma-
chinery.

Except where climate permits it would be difficult to cultivate

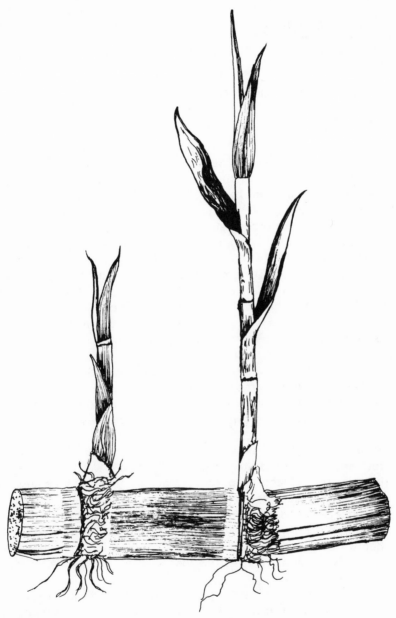

Thou has bought me no sweet cane with money.
(Isaiah 43:24)

sugar cane in a biblical garden. Nevertheless it is noteworthy that the Second Isaiah was aware of this giant perennial grass and included it in his writings which fell between 549 and 538 B.C.

CUCUMBER

Cucumis sativus
Biblical term: Cucumbers

WHILE WANDERING IN THE DESERT, the children of Israel yearned for the vegetables that grew in abundance in Egypt (Numbers 11:5). They had dwelt as slaves in the Nile Valley for hundreds of years, yet the desolate wilderness of the Sinai Peninsula had dulled their memories of deliverance from oppression. Dissatisfied with the manna God provided (Exodus 16:15–21), they expressed their grievances to their leader Moses.

Long before Old Testament times, cucumbers were cultivated in the warmer climates of the Old World and probably originated in northern India. The familiar garden kind, *Cucumis sativus,* was well known and enjoyed in Egypt as a vegetable and salad plant. When the Israelites settled in Palestine, they began to raise their own cucumbers. Today in Israel cucumbers grow in level fields by the acre, wherever water is plentiful. In summer, juicy and refreshing cucumbers form an important part of the diet. The natives usually eat them raw with a barley cake or some other sort of bread to make up a meal. Pickling of cucumbers is an ancient custom also practiced in modern times.

As the cucumbers ripened on the vines, an owner erected a temporary shelter in the center of his field where a watchman lived and guarded the valuable crop from marauders. These fragile huts, built of branches and leaves, were left to disintegrate at the end of the harvesting. Isaiah compared Judah to an isolated "lodge in a garden of cucumbers" (1:8). Sennacherib the Assyrian had devastated all of Judah with the exception of Jerusalem, which King Hezekiah did not surrender (II Kings 18:13–15). Thus the royal city stood aloft and forlorn, surrounded by ruin.

The cucumber is an annual sprawling vine widely cultivated for its crisp, fleshy fruit. It has succulent trailing stems and stalked hairy leaves with 3 to 5 pointed lobes. Branched tendrils on the stems make it possible to train the plant to climb up a fence or trellis. The short-stalked, bell-shaped, yellow flowers are pollenized by bees. Principal types of cucumbers are the long, smooth, dark green slicing kinds, the small, heavy-bearing pickling kinds, and the rounded, yellow, sweet-flavored lemon or apple types. Dwarf bush varieties have been

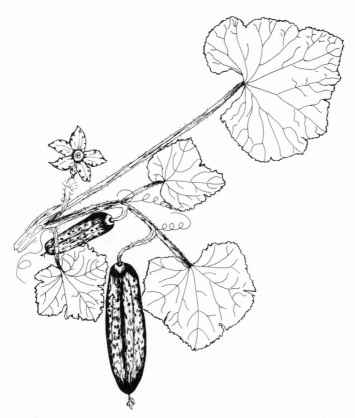

*And the daughter of Zion is left as a cottage in a vineyard, as a
lodge in a garden of cucumbers, as a besieged city.*
(Isaiah 1:8)

bred especially for miniature gardens or container growing and bear
cucumbers excellent for slicing. One hybrid space saver will grow in a
pot on a sunny windowsill.

Cucumbers need considerable moisture, warmth, and a light, well-
drained soil to produce healthy vines. They are more sensitive to frost
than most vegetables, requiring a frost-free period of 75 to 90 days.
Seeds of outdoor varieties may be sown indoors or directly in the
ground when the weather is thoroughly settled. A second seeding in
four or five weeks will assure a summer-long harvest.

Cucumber vines can fill numerous spots in a biblical garden. Outdoor varieties may be allowed to ramble over the ground or be given a
support to climb upon to save space. Bush types planted in containers find favor in gracing a patio, balcony, or a hanging basket. The
delectable cucumbers will provide pickles of various sorts, with the
remainder eaten raw in salads or like sticks of celery.

MELONS

MANY COMMENTATORS BELIEVE THE "melons" mentioned in Numbers 11:5 include the muskmelon and the watermelon, due to the fact that both kinds were cultivated in Egypt before the Israelites were delivered from bondage. They are still widely grown in Egypt as well as Israel for their sweet taste and thirst-quenching qualities. In Egypt, the watermelon supplies food, drink, and medicine. The seeds are popular roasted and salted. On soil that was softened and fertilized by the annual overflowing of the Nile, such food crops flourished with little attention.

Both types of melons are regarded as fruits, but are treated as vegetables in the garden. They are usually planted in hills or mounds, consuming considerable space. A long, frost-free period, strong sunshine, with a minimum daytime temperature of no less than 80 degrees F. are essential. Other demands are a somewhat sandy, well-drained soil, a constant supply of moisture, and heavy applications of fertilizer. When seed is planted directly in the ground, the soil must be warm and frost danger past. Seeds sown indoors in peat pots and later transplanted to the garden guarantee an earlier crop.

MUSKMELON

Cucumis melo
Biblical term: Melons

THIS MELON-TYPE ANNUAL OF THE cucumber family is probably a native of Central Asia. From it has sprung all the cultivated melons with the exception of the watermelon. This soft, hairy vine, with rough round to oval leaves, bears tendrils but seldom climbs. Yellow, bell-shaped flowers, about an inch wide, develop in a leaf-axil. The small, round fruits of the true muskmelon, *C. melo*, have hard, scaly, rough skins, but the flesh is succulent, juicy, and sweet tasting. Only rarely is it grown in the United States. Our principal varieties consist of the cantaloupes, honey-balls, honeydews, casabas, cranshaws, and Persians. They vary greatly in shape, size, skin texture, and color of flesh. Each carries its own distinct flavor. When ripe, the melons are aromatic and the stems slip off easily from the vines.

*We remember the fish, which we did eat in Egypt freely;
the cucumbers, and the melons, and the leeks,
and the onions, and the garlick.*

(Numbers 11:5)

WATERMELON

Citrullus vulgaris
Biblical term: Melons

CLOSELY RELATED TO THE MUSKMELON, the watermelon is native to tropical Africa. Egyptian paintings portraying it date back from the time of the pyramids. The prostrate plant is a long-running, hairy, annual vine with branched tendrils. Leaves are large, broad, and divided into segments, while the light yellow flowers form singly in the leaf axils. Watermelons may be oblong or round, glossy dark green, light or grayish green in color, with or without attractive stripes or mottlings. Their crisp, watery flesh ranges in color from rich dark red to pink. To test for ripeness, slap the side of the melon with the open palm of your hand. The reverberating sound should be deep and resonant. In parched lands, such as Egypt and Palestine, watermelons serve as an alternative to water.

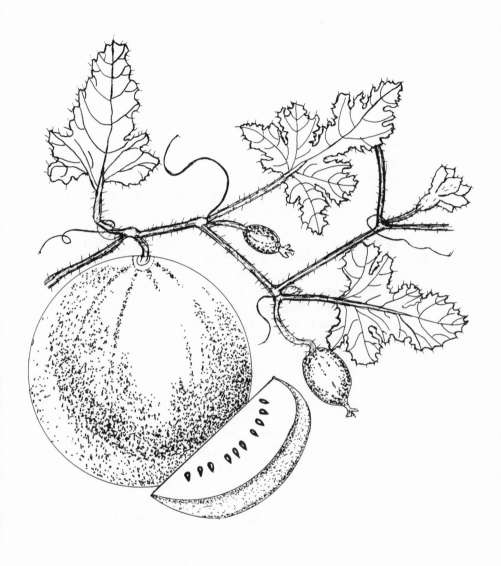

*We remember the fish, which we did eat in Egypt freely;
the cucumbers, and the melons. . . .*
(Numbers 11:5)

LEEK

Allium porrum
Biblical term: Leeks

AMONG THE VEGETABLES THE ISRAELITES sighed for as sojourners in the wilderness were "the leeks" (Numbers 11:5). The plant was commonly grown in Egypt in the time of the pharaohs and continues to be up to the present. The Israelites cultivated leeks upon settling in Palestine, where they retain their popularity. Delicately flavored members of the onion family, they are used to replace the stronger tasting onion in seasoning soups, stews, and various other dishes. Leeks are also eaten raw or sliced in salads. Often the base and leaves are lightly boiled or steamed and served as a cooked vegetable.

The bottom part of the leek resembles a fat, cylindrical, green onion in not having a distinct bulb. Its flat, broad, juicy, coarse leaves overlap each other to form a swollen, stemlike base. As a biennial, it blooms the second year on the end of a stem which may reach a height of 2 to 3 feet. The small white flowers appear in a large, ball-like cluster, similar to those of an onion. From the flowers come viable seeds.

Leeks require rich, deep, loamy soil, constant moisture, and a substantial amount of sunlight. In cold-winter areas, the seeds must be sown indoors in early spring and the plants set out in June or July. Elsewhere the seeds may be planted directly in the ground when the soil is workable. After the plants have made considerable growth, the earth is drawn up around the fat stems as they lengthen. This is done to make the bottoms white and to induce a better flavor. Harvesting begins in the fall and the leeks dug as needed. In the coldest areas the remaining plants should be dug up in the fall and stored in boxes of soil in a cool, dark, but frost-free location. Leeks are suitable for container gardening, either permanently or temporarily.

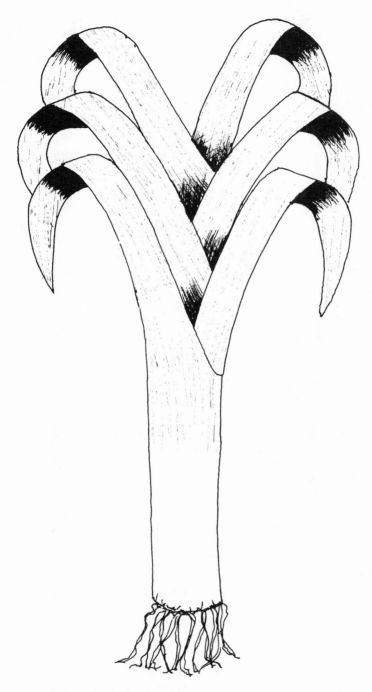

We remember . . . the leeks. . . .
  (Numbers 11:5)

ONION

Allium cepa
Biblical term: Onions

THE ONIONS MENTIONED IN NUMBERS 11:5 were probably a variety of the onion *Allium cepa,* known to us as Egyptian onion, multiplier, or tree onion. While its native home is traditionally western Asia, there is no question as to its cultivation and use in Egypt during the time of Moses. Builders of the Great Pyramid consumed enormous quantities of onions, garlic, and radishes. Onions were so highly esteemed in Egypt that they were represented more than any other plant in tomb paintings. Ancient Egyptians worshipped this onion. They have been described by ancient writers as mild, sweet-tasting, and more easily digested than any other onion. In Eastern countries, the poor have lived on sliced onions and bread or onion soup. The more affluent enjoyed the small, pungent bulbs as a relish, in stews, or to flavor roasts.

An Egyptian onion is unique not only because it is a perennial, but also because of its habit of forming annual crops of bulblets atop 3 foot stems and sometimes among the greenish-white flower clusters. As the mother bulb grows larger, the clustered bulblets increase in size and number. Often the larger bulblets grow more bulblets higher up on a new stem, earning the plant the common name of tree onion. The bulblets may be planted to produce green onions for pulling and eating fresh. The mother onion remains in the ground from year to year until finally deteriorating.

Bulblets of Egyptian onions are rather difficult to find, but once obtained another supply is never needed. In mild winter climates, the bulbs are planted in the fall. In other regions, they are set out in early spring as soon as the soil is workable. A crop of onions can be expected within a year of planting. They grow best in a loose, rich, fast-draining soil in a sunny location. Soil must be kept moist at all times. Hardy and easy to grow, they quickly establish themselves. A trellis or stake to hold the stems erect will hasten ripening. These onions may be grown indoors in pots if strong light is available or rotated between indoors and out.

The small, mild Egyptian onion is used chopped in salads or sandwiches, made into pickles, or dried and used to flavor roasts and stews. Where space is limited, this onion is an excellent substitute for the commonly grown annual onion.

We remember . . . the onions. . . .
(Numbers 11:5)

GARLIC

Allium sativum
Biblical term: Garlick

IN THE AUTHORIZED VERSION, THE garlic of Numbers 11:5 is spelled "garlick." This onionlike plant of great antiquity originated in Central Asia. Earliest Sanskrit writings show that garlic was grown long before the Bible was written. For centuries the strongly scented vegetable was cultivated in Egypt to furnish part of the diet of the workers on the pyramids. The ancients also used the juice of the bulbous root to control internal and external diseases. Garlic was so important in the lives of the wandering Israelites that they craved it. In Palestine and other Mediterranean countries, garlic is a favorite among all classes of people. Few savory dishes are prepared without additions of chopped or crushed garlic cloves. Less generous amounts are generally used in the United States to flavor salad dressings, stews, soups, and roasts. Many of our processed foods contain a hint of garlic.

The common garlic is a hardy perennial, with slender, straplike leaves growing from 1 to 2 feet high. During early summer the plant sends up a slim stalk topped by small globular clusters of tiny pinkish flowers. These sterile flowers should be picked off as soon as they form. Each plant produces a single bulb composed of a number of bulblets called cloves, which are wrapped closely together in a pinkish-white, papery skin.

Garlic seed is seldom available, so the garlic bulb is divided, and the cloves are pressed into the ground about 2 inches deep and 9 inches apart. They should be situated in a sunny location and in a well-cultivated, rich, fast-draining soil in early fall or in early spring where winters are severe. Regular watering during dry periods promotes faster growth. Harvest begins when the green foliage turns brown in late summer. After pulling the bulbs from the ground and removing the tops and roots, leave them in the sun for a few days to dry before storing them in a cool, airy place. Garlic bulbs can be left in the ground over winter if well-mulched.

It is possible to grow a garlic clove in a 4 inch pot on a bright, sunny windowsill. Planted halfway in the soil and watered moderately, it is likely to produce offsets which can be separated and propagated by themselves. Garlic leaves have a less pungent odor than the cloves, and these can be utilized to enrich cookery.

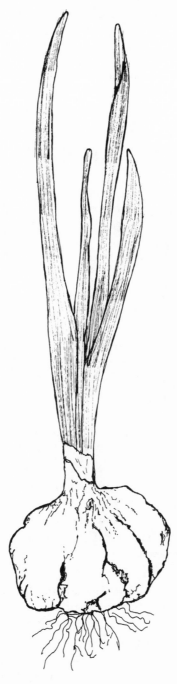

We remember . . . the garlic. . . .
(Numbers 11:5)

PART 3

Herbs and Spices

Herbs and spices were collected or cultivated in Bible lands for practical purposes rather than for mere ornaments. Foliage, seeds, and roots were the main harvest, for from these were captured the heavy fragrances of essential oils used in making perfumes, beauty aids, and ingredients for embalming and religious ceremonies. Some rare spices, such as gums, were imported from Arabia and India. By far the most important use for herbs was to furnish material for medicines. But the ancients well knew the virtues of various aromatic herbs to spark up dull foods. Other herbs were grown commercially either for their fibers or for colors used in dyeing.

Private herb gardens were held in high esteem by the rich of Palestine. Solomon maintained several kinds of herb gardens (Song of Solomon 4:12–16, 6:11), obtaining the seeds or plants through his merchant traders. King Ahab of Israel unlawfully seized a prosperous vineyard adjoining his property in order to institute an herb garden close to his palace (I Kings 21:1–28). Traditionally, a wall or thick hedge enclosed an herb garden: otherwise the wind would carry off the delightful fragrance of the flowers.

Today herbs and spices are grown in American gardens largely for seasoning foods and for the luscious smells of the flowers and leaves, hence combining practicality with adornment. They may be cultivated in a separate garden plot, with herbs in sufficient quantities to dry for winter use or gifts. A space in the flower border or vegetable garden is enough for a few plants. Smaller types will function planted in a windowbox or a pot placed on a kitchen sill. Here the advantages are accessibility and easy care.

BITTER HERBS

As God had commanded, the Israelites celebrated their liberation from Egypt with a Passover feast, even in the Sinai wilderness (Numbers 9:5). Every family served five bitter herbs along with roast lamb and bread made without yeast. The rite represents the bitter slavery from which God delivered the Israelites. Various herbs have been used by Jews for this purpose through the centuries. Today horseradish is generally used in the United States, but it was unknown in Bible times. The following herbs may well have been employed in ancient days, for they were and still are common in Egypt and Palestine.

CHICORY

Cichorium intybus
Biblical term: Bitter herbs

CHICORY, CALLED ALSO SUCCORY, grew plentifully as a wild plant in ancient Egypt, and the first edible varieties were developed there and in Syria. Egyptians consumed huge amounts of chicory, naming it the "liver's friend" because the herb was thought to purify the blood and liver. It was eaten chopped, ground, and boiled. Eating the tender young leaves with meat and bread was probably a custom the Israelites acquired from the Egyptians during their bondage.

Wild chicory is abundant along roadsides in North America, but is cultivated as a farm crop in some sections. In home gardens the plant is grown chiefly for its young leaves which have only a slightly bitter taste. Mild and nippy, they highlight mixed green salads or substitute for spinach when cooked. The fleshy white roots are dried, ground, and roasted to serve as an alternative to coffee or a component to intensify the flavor of coffee.

From the long taproot of chicory ascends a rigid, multibranched, hairy stem 3 to 6 feet high. The edible leaves around the base look much like those of the dandelion to which it is related. The fragrant flower heads are bright blue, measure nearly 2 inches across, and bloom on long, stiff stems from July until frost-killed. After the foliage dies down, the roots may be dug from the ground and made ready for forcing. They are forced into growth by planting them in compost and by storing in a warm place. Forcing causes the new growth to become white, crisp, sweet, and tender. The shoots are excellent to use in raw winter salads and for boiling.

A hardy perennial herb, chicory prefers rich soil containing plenty of humus, much sunshine, and moisture. Seeds are sown in rows in the spring, germinating in about two weeks. Within a month the plants are ready for thinning and for use in salads. Keeping the plants spaced 18 inches apart will allow the remaining roots room to expand.

Chicory can be grown in a pot for indoor gardening. The long taproot makes it difficult to transplant without injury, so a large, deep pot is necessary. Two or three seeds are planted to a pot, kept well watered, and given a sunny site by a window. Top growth is trimmed back to induce branching.

*The fourteenth day of the second month at even they shall keep
it, and eat it with unleavened bread and bitter herbs.*
(Numbers 9:11)

DANDELION

Taraxacum officinale
Biblical term: Bitter herbs

THE DANDELION, THOUGH OF EUROPEAN origin, is naturalized in most parts of the world, growing in meadows, waste places, on damp or dry sandy soil, and often on cultivated ground. A perennial herb with a bitter taste and related to chicory, it was used in ancient times as a vegetable, and the root as a medicine believed to cure most ailments. Known since the time of Moses, it is presumed to be one of the bitter herbs eaten by the Israelites while observing the ritual of the Passover (Numbers 9:11).

Since ancients times, the young and tender leaves of the dandelion have been included in raw salads and the thick dark-green leaves boiled as potherbs. Bitterness in the older leaves is removed by cooking them in at least two changes of water. They are inordinately nourishing, containing more food value than lettuce or spinach. The dried roots have been extensively employed by doctors as a diuretic, tonic, stimulant, and for liver disorders. A light golden wine made from the crushed flower heads has been through the ages extolled in song and story. More recently, the dried and roasted roots are ground and made into a bitter, coffeelike beverage or used to replace chicory in coffee.

Dandelions obtain their name from the French word meaning lion's teeth, in an allusion to the basal rosette of toothlike lobes of the leaves that appear in the spring. Their long, thick taproots cause difficulty in uprooting them. From April to August, bright golden-yellow flower heads bloom atop smooth, leafless, hollow, and numerous stalks. These should be pinched off before the globe-shaped clusters of seeds form and are dispersed by the wind. In all parts of the plant a bitter milky fluid is present.

Wild dandelions can be utilized for propagation and under cultivation will produce larger plants. In areas where they form few leaves, it is best to use seed packet varieties. The seeds are sown as a spring or fall crop in a semishady spot. The richer the soil, the more tender the leaves will be. Once the leaves have matured, the outer ones can be picked off to add pungency to raw salads or to boil as greens. The vigorous plants will soon bear new leaves from the tops of the taproots.

A young wild dandelion can be dug and removed to a deep pot

And they shall eat the flesh in that night, roast with fire, and unleavened bread; and with bitter herbs they shall eat it.
(Exodus 12:8)

for indoor gardening. Its requirements are a rich soil kept well watered and a partially sunny location. The leaves may be picked off as needed.

ENDIVE

Cichorium endivia
Biblical term: Herb

ENDIVE, AN ANNUAL OR BIENNIAL HERB closely related to chicory, is, according to some authorities, indigenous to Egypt. Wherever its origin, it grew in ancient Egypt and has been used since earliest times as salad greens. Normally intensely bitter tasting, it was most likely one of the bitter herbs eaten at the Feast of the Passover (Exodus 12:8; Numbers 9:11).

The plant differs from chicory in that the numerous basal leaves are curled, less deeply lobed, and covered somewhat with a whitish powder. The narrow upper leaves clasp the leafy stem which grows 2 to 3 feet high. Below the clustered, purple flower heads is a series of leafy bracts that exceed the head in size.

A number of modern varieties of endive are milder and more tender than the original kind. The broad-leaf Bavarian, known as escarole, is considered the best for culinary purposes. It has broad, slightly curly leaves like those of lettuce and, when mature, forms a nearly flat rosette of leaves up to 18 inches across.

The blanching of all varieties of endive is important in order to prevent the development of the usual bitterness and toughness of the leaves. After the plants reach maturity, gather the outer leaves around the inner ones and secure with string or a rubberband. Within three weeks the green, succulent, center leaves bleach to creamy white. They are crisp, tender, contain only a delicately pungent taste, and serve as a substitute for lettuce.

Seeds are sown indoors in the spring for an early crop or outdoors in midsummer to perform as a biennial. In three months the plants are ready for harvesting. Endive will thrive wherever lettuce can be grown, requiring a rich, well-drained soil, a sunny site, and watering when the ground becomes dry. Composting will keep the soil cool in hot weather and help the plants to withstand prolonged frost.

Endive can be grown easily in a container, either indoors or out.

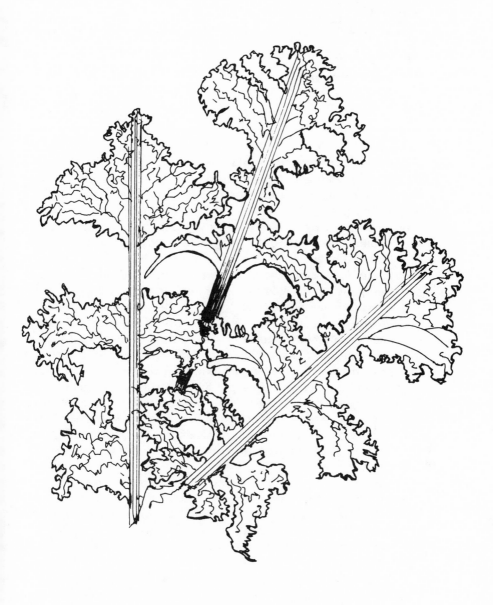

. . . the Lord God made the earth and the heavens . . . and every herb of the field before it grew.

(Genesis 2:4–5)

LETTUCE

Lactuca sativa
Biblical term: Herb

ALTHOUGH BELIEVED TO HAVE ORIGINATED in Asia, a weedy kind of lettuce grew wild in ancient Egypt where it was introduced to the Israelites. It is a prickly annual herb known as *Lactuca scariola,* growing nearly 5 feet tall, with bitter tasting, prickly margined leaves of bluish green. The pale yellow flower heads form on tall, upright, many-branched stems. Related to chicory, dandelion, and endive, lettuce was probably among the bitter herbs eaten with the Pascal lamb (Exodus 12:5; Numbers 11:9). Our present-day mild-flavored lettuce is thought to have been developed from this milky-juiced wild species that still thrives in the wild in the greater part of the world.

Today there are several hundred varieties of lettuce, all holding prominence throughout the year as the prime ingredient of salads. Most commonly cultivated in home gardens are various forms of loosehead lettuce, *L. sativa,* so called for the loose rosette of curled, finely cut, green leaves, averaging 8 to 12 inches across. It will grow anywhere in the United States, producing a constant crop of leaves. The crisp, fresh, outer leaves are pinched off at the base as they mature, while the inner leaves continue to replace them the whole season. Lettuce plants can endure several degrees of frost, but midsummer heat will cause production of tall flower stalks that prevent the formation of heads.

Looseleaf lettuce is unmistakably a cool weather crop, to be grown in early spring, late summer, or early fall. Like most lettuce, it favors an enriched, well-worked, sandy soil, with an abundance of moisture to induce quick growth. Seeds may be sown directly in the garden as soon as the ground can be worked. As the plants grow, they must be thinned to allow ample room for expansion.

One petite type of lettuce named "Tom Thumb" is invaluable where space is limited. It makes crisp, compact heads useful for individual salad servings, either whole, halved, or quartered, and it will reach maturity in a windowbox or a 4 inch pot. Preferring cool weather, the seeds should be planted in the spring, then again in late summer and fall.

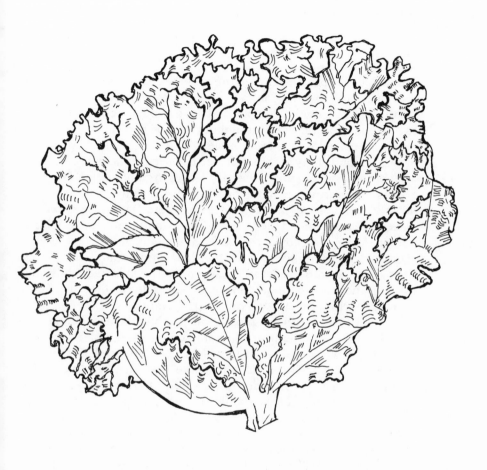

He causeth the grass to grow for the cattle,
and herb for the service of man.
(Psalms 104:14)

SORREL

Rumex acetosella
Biblical term: Herb

THE SORREL, OR DOCK, KNOWN to the Israelites (Exodus 9:25; Numbers 9:11) was probably the common sheep's sorrel, *Rumex acetosella,* a small, erect, perennial herb native to Eurasia and found naturalized as a strong-growing weed throughout Europe and North America. A plant of great antiquity, it was familiar to the Egyptians in the time of Moses. Its long, narrow, arrow-shaped basal leaves have a sour, somewhat bitter taste. Egyptians used the leaves in combination with other greens to improve their flavor. Numerous dainty, reddish-green flowers hang in long, branching clusters from May to July, to be replaced by brownish-red seeds. As the seeds mature the leaves redden. Roman doctors employed the leaves as a medicine.

Garden sorrel, *R. acetosa,* another herb of great antiquity, is less weedy and has larger leaves than sheep's sorrel. It is frequently cultivated in modern home gardens as a vegetable for greens. The extremely nutritious leaves contain large quantities of vitamins A and C. Like all sorrels, it has a reputation as a blood cleanser and for a warming effect on the heart. Roughly chopped fresh leaves give a sharp, tart flavor to salads and omelets. They are used as a main ingredient in preparing sauces to serve with fish and meat. The chopped leaves are also added to vegetable or meat soups a few minutes before serving. Sorrels should be used sparingly, for their strong oxalic content can cause injury to the kidneys.

An open, rich, sandy soil and an abundance of sunshine are the main needs of the hardy sorrels. For new plants the roots are divided in spring or started from seed sown in April. The seedlings should be transplanted to 12 inches apart. It will take about a dozen plants to produce enough leaves for regular use. They must be kept well watered during dry weather to insure a bountiful supply. If you pinch out the flower heads as they form, the plants will yield crops for several years.

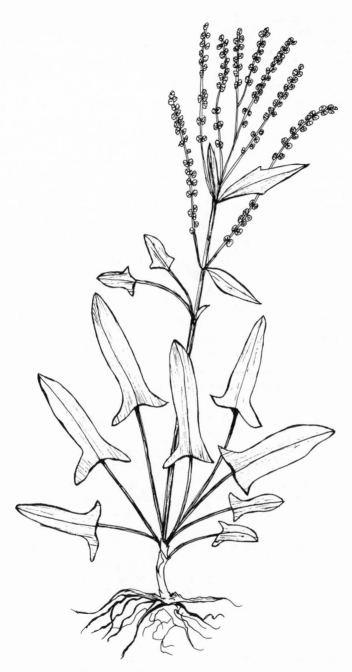

. . . and the hail smote every herb of the field,
and brake every tree of the field.
(Exodus 9:25)

WATERCRESS

Nasturtium officinale
Biblical term: Herb

FROM EARLY TIMES, WATERCRESS, *Nasturtium officinale,* has been appreciated for its biting, pungent taste and health-providing qualities. Though a native of Europe and Asia, it is widely naturalized throughout the world. It grows along riverbanks, shallow streams, and wet-lying meadows, or in cold, quietly flowing water. The allusion to bitter herbs in the Bible (Exodus 12:8; Deuteronomy 32:2) may have included the perennial watercress, for it was a common food plant of early Egyptians, who used the leaves to sharpen the flavor of green salads. The Persians regarded watercress as a valuable stimulant for children. Up until the nineteenth century, watercress grew so plentifully in the wild state that it was needless to cultivate it in home gardens or for market purposes.

The deep green, glossy leaves of watercress are composed of a few to several small, fleshy, rounded leaflets, with a larger terminal leaflet. These arise from rather weak, hollow stems growing to twelve inches tall. Leaves of watercress have a high iron content, are rich in vitamins, and afford an excellent remedy for scurvy. The leaves may be cooked like spinach, but they produce a peppery taste and are best boiled with spinach. Served in mayonnaise sandwiches, as a garnish for salads, or chopped in cream cheese, they lend a delicious tangy flavor. Sometimes the hot-tasting seeds that develop from the elongated clusters of tiny white flowers are ground and added to mustard.

Home gardeners who have a brook, pool, or pond can readily root watercress by inserting broken-off stems in the water without attachment to soil. If no such source is available, this hardy semiaquatic herb will take root in a shaded location as long as it is kept constantly wet. Any sandy soil will do, but the addition of organic material and a mulch gives better results.

Watercress seed is sown outdoors from early spring to fall, with each successive planting producing a crop inside a month's time. It will stay green until damaged by frost. The plants may be dug and grown indoors in a shallow pot, set in a saucer of water. Or, if stems are placed in a glass of water, they will produce roots within a period of several days. Just snip off the leaves when needed. Starts of watercress can be gathered from the wild or bought in grocery stores.

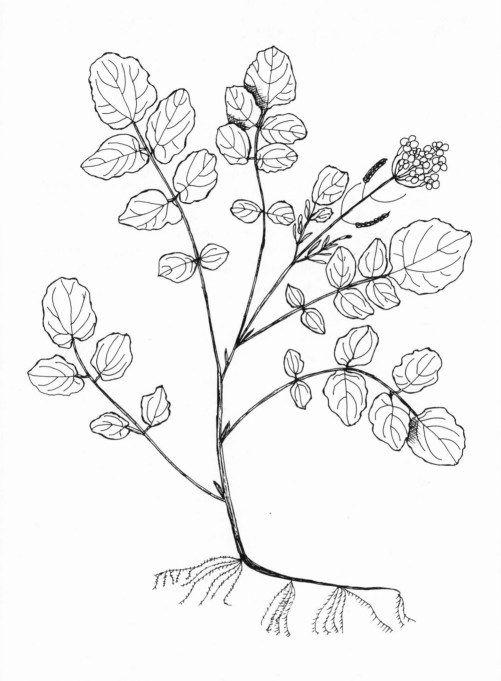

My doctrine shall drop . . . as the small rain upon the tender herb, and as the showers upon the grass.
(Deuteronomy 32:2)

TITHING HERBS

THE MOSAIC CODE OF LAWS prescribed the tithing of grain and other possessions (Deuteronomy 14:22–23). In New Testament times tithing was strictly observed by the Pharisees (Luke 18:12), who defined grain as including all wild herbs commonly found in Palestine (Matthew 23:23). Jesus denounced these religious leaders for their lack of concern for the more important matters of charity and spirituality (Micah 6:8). Following are descriptions of herbs mentioned in the Matthew passage.

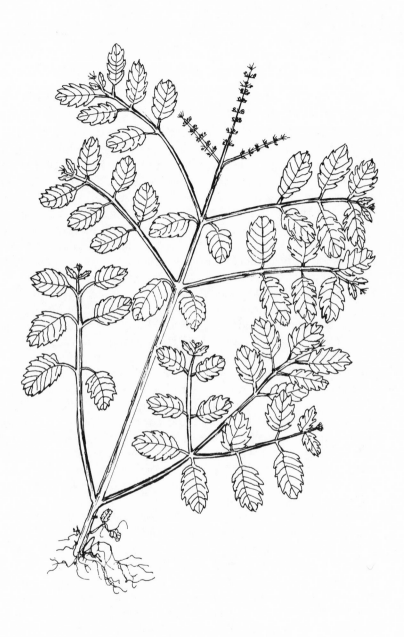

MINT

Mentha longifolia
Biblical term: Mint

SEVERAL VARIETIES OF MINT ARE FOUND in Palestine and Syria, but the mint of the New Testament (Matthew 23:23; Luke 11:42) was probably horsemint, *Mentha longifolia*. It grows wild in ditches, damp fields, and along watersides, but was also cultivated in biblical days to add piquancy to food, for medicinal purposes, and for worship. Mint was often strewn on the floors of synagogues to suppress bad odors. Nowadays it is one of the bitter herbs eaten at the Jewish Passover feast.

Horsemint is an erect, strong-scented perennial. Its silvery-gray, silky-haired, aromatic leaves, to 2 inches long, are lance shaped and toothed. Its branched or unbranched stout stems grow 20 to 30 inches high. The small rose or lilac flowers are arranged in clusters, forming on terminal spikes in midsummer. Like other mints, horsemint is a rampant grower and, if not curbed, its trailing suckers will soon assume possession of a garden. Frequent cutting or confining the roots in a bottomless bucket sunk in the soil will prevent rapid spreading. For securing the soil on slopes, the running roots have great value. Horsemint can be grown indoors in a shallow container on a windowsill. Pruning will increase its attractiveness.

All mints grow best outdoors in partial shade where cool, damp conditions prevail. The soil should contain plenty of humus, since mints are avaricious feeders. At the end of the growing season, it is a good idea to cut the stems down to the ground and cover the bed with a layer of mulch. Mints are easily grown from seed, or propagated from runners which are rooted at the joints. The cuttings will root in moist sand or a glass of water.

More than thirty mint varieties exist in the North Temperate Zone, each contributing a somewhat different flavor. They are cultivated for the essential oils which produce an intense, fragrant aroma. A popular use today is in flavoring jellies and sauces to accompany lamb. The leaves and flowering tops give a refreshing fragrance to home-brewed tea made to relieve headaches and to promote sleep. Oil extracted from the plants is employed in medical prescriptions, either to disguise a disagreeable taste or to aid digestion. Mints offer a distinctive savor to fruit salads and cooked vegetables and are used to enhance cakes, candies, frostings, and sherbets. The leaves can be gathered and dried for later use. Through the ages mints have served remarkably similar purposes.

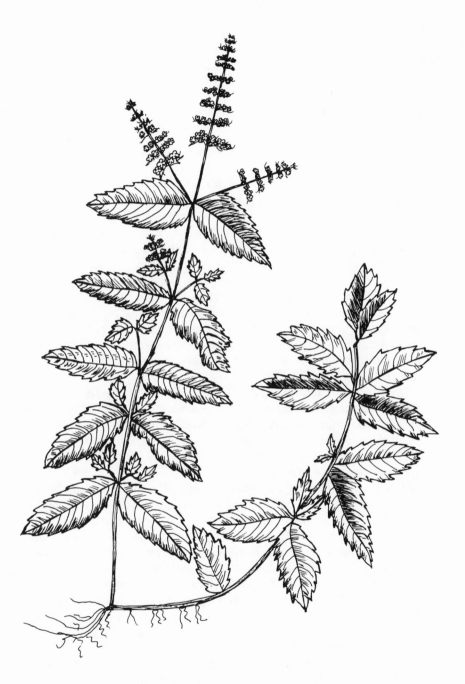

Woe unto you, scribes and Pharisees,
hypocrites! For ye pay tithe of mint.
(Matthew 23:23)

DILL

Anethum graveolens
Biblical term: Anise

MODERN BIBLICAL BOTANISTS CONCUR that the translation of "anise" in the Authorized Version should be rendered as dill. It is a pungent herb indigenous to the Near East and Palestine, and cultivated on the plains of Sharon. The aromatic seeds are ground and eaten as a sour condiment or used for seasoning cakes. Dill was and still is valued for its medicinal properties, sometimes being used in the form of dill-water to relieve gas pains. Early Romans used the fragrant leaves to make wreaths to honor heroes, and to decorate banquet halls. Talmudic writings indicate that the seeds, stems, and leaves were subject to tithe. Thus, dill was among the herbs from which the Pharisees punctiliously paid tithes in the temple. Jesus pointed out that they were guilty of ignoring more serious obligations specified in the Mosaic code (Matthew 23:23).

Dill is an annual growing 2 to 3 feet high, with attractive feathery, finely dissected, blue-green leaves resembling those of anise. It has flat-topped, umbrellalike clusters of tiny, bright yellow flowers, from which emerge the flat, aromatic fruit, or seed. Fresh or home-cured dill is by far richer in taste than the commercial product and is therefore indispensable in an herb garden.

With the exception of the roots, all parts of the plant are edible. The fresh young foliage is harvested to give a strong flavor to sauces served with fish and meat dishes, or, when finely chopped, to impart a distinctive taste to cottage cheese, cream cheese, or yogurt. Fresh leaves are also palatable if sprinkled over steaks and chops, in soups and stews, and in cooking water for vegetables. Dry or green seeds, leaves, and flowering heads give a spicy tang to pickles, relishes, and vinegar. The dried crushed seeds are prized in soups and salads, and to replace salt in butter, margarine, breads, and vegetables. Modern herbalists recommend dill for the treatment of stomach ailments and kidney disorders.

Dill requires a sunny location, along with a well-drained soil and plenty of humus. Seeds should be sown where the plants are to grow, because dill is difficult to transplant but will reseed itself year after year. For a continuous crop, the seeds must be sown several times during spring and summer. Seedlings need to be thinned to 18 inches

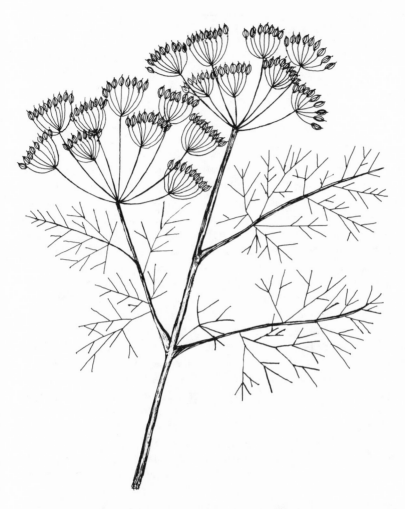

*. . . ye pay tithe of . . . anise . . . and have omitted the
weightier matters of the law.*
(Matthew 23:23)

apart, and spindly plants given stakes for supports. The entire plant is
harvested when the seeds become ripe. Cut the stems just above
ground level. Tie the stems in small bunches, and hang them heads
down in a dry, warm, airy place. If hung above paper-lined trays, the
seeds can be collected as they drop and stored separately.

For indoor gardening, sow the dill seeds directly into a 6 inch pot.
Set the pot in bright sunlight and keep the soil moist. The plants will
not produce seeds, but by sowing four times a year, you will always
have a supply of leaves for cooking.

CUMIN, CUMINUM

Cuminum cyminum
Biblical term: Cumin

ANOTHER PRODUCT TITHED BY THE Pharisees under the category of grain was cumin (Matthew 23:23). This low-growing herb native to the Mediterranean region has been cultivated extensively in Palestine since the days of Isaiah. It is best known for its strongly aromatic and pungent seeds which the Jews relished in their unleavened bread. The seed in the Near East is used as a condiment and spice to season cakes and stews as well as in breadmaking. As a seasoning it has been given a role corresponding to that of pepper and was one of the most important spices in Roman cookery. Cumin seeds, resembling those of caraway in appearance and taste, have long been acclaimed for their medicinal value, paralleling dill in digestive properties. In a parable, the prophet Isaiah explains the farmer's method of beating out the small, tender seeds with a stick, consequently preventing the loss caused by any other means of harvesting (Isaiah 28:23–29).

Cumin is a dainty, half-hardy annual, growing scarcely 6 inches high, with a slim, well-branched stem extending from the base. The leaves are long, slender, and finely dissected. Clusters of tiny, white or pinkish flowers form at the tops of the branches. When the bristly, rounded seeds turn brown in the fall, the plants are pulled up, the seeds thoroughly dried, and the cleaned seeds stored in airtight containers in order to preserve their freshness and strength.

Today the greatest use of cumin is as an ingredient in chili powder, curry powder, chutney, and pickles. The ground seeds are also used in sausages, cheeses, and spaghetti sauces. Often cumin is called for in recipes for soup, broiled lamb, fish, and rice. An infusion made from the seeds is occasionally imbibed as a tea to aid digestion. Oil distilled from the seeds flavors liqueurs.

Seeds of cumin should be sown in the ground where the plants are to mature and the seedlings thinned out gradually to 6 inches apart. Place them in well-drained soil in an open, sunny spot in the garden. As natives of hot, dry regions, they will tolerate the driest conditions. Cumin can be grown readily in a container by a sunny window.

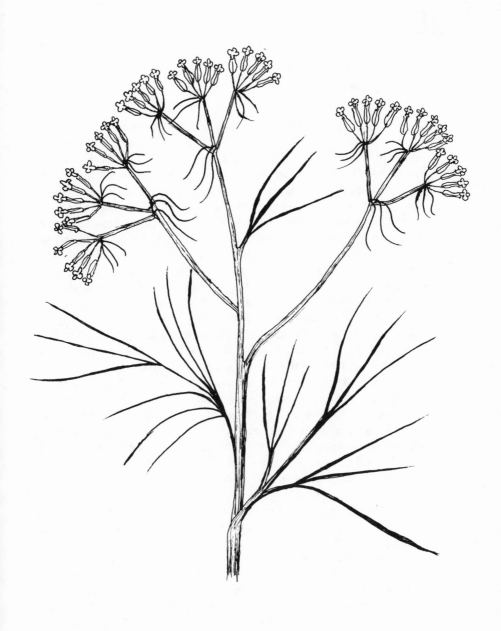

. . . the fitches are beaten out with a staff,
and the cummin with a rod.
  (Isaiah 28:27)

RUE

Ruta graveolens
Biblical term: Rue

RUE IS A PRETTY BUT BITTER HERB which is mentioned only once in the Bible, when Jesus rebuked the Pharisees for the hypocrisy manifested in their religious practices (Luke 11:42). The natural habitat of rue is the Mediterranean region where it grows in ditches, on hillsides, and beside old walls. It was cultivated in Palestine during the ministry of Jesus for use in medicine and as flavoring for food. To the ancient Greeks and Romans, rue represented protection against diseases. They would strew it on floors of public buildings and carry bouquets of the plant in their hands. Pliny lists eighty-four remedies containing rue. It was once called the "herb of grace" because of the association of its name with repentance. Rue earned considerable distinction in the past as a stimulative and an antiseptic and is employed in modern veterinary medicine.

Rue is a somewhat woody, bushlike perennial, growing 2 to 3 feet high, with aromatic, divided, and fernlike leaves of blue green, which, in warmer sections of the United States, remain on the plant well into winter. In its second year of growth, small, greenish-yellow flowers with buttonlike green centers hang in loose clusters from atop upright stems. Both leaves and flowers emit a rather musty, pungent odor. The graceful branches and brown, lobed seed capsules are decorative in flower arrangements, while the dry seed clusters find use in wreaths and swags.

Strong in mineral salts, the leaves make an excellent tonic in the form of rue tea. The chopped leaves, used sparingly, give a hint of bitterness when placed between cheese, cress, or lettuce in sandwiches. They help round out the taste of such vegetables as asparagus, eggplant, and peas.

Rue likes a well-drained, limy soil, full sun, and is tolerant of moisture. New plants are easily raised from seed sown in spring or early summer, but are propagated more rapidly from cuttings taken in summer and rooted in sandy soil. Root division is another possible method of propagation. Due to their bushiness, the plants should stand 12 inches or more apart. Used in the back of a border or as a low hedge, they contribute beauty as well as utility value.

This biblical herb is one of the best pot plants to grow indoors, for there the leaves stay green throughout the year in any locality. But it seldom, if ever, flowers indoors, even when set in strong sunlight.

But woe unto you, Pharisees! for ye tithe
mint and rue and all manner of herbs.
(Luke 11:42)

OTHER HERBS AND SPICES

THE BIBLE ABOUNDS in allusions to herbs and spices. They constituted a requisite part of daily living and therefore were highly prized in ancient times. Obtainable from trees, smaller plants and roots, they were often gathered from the wild, but were sometimes cultivated. For example, the little blue-flowered flax plant was cultivated in Egypt and Palestine for its strong vegetable fibers, which were used in weaving linen. The ripened seeds were "boiled" for their oil content (Exodus 9:31). This crop plant antedated cotton as the leading textile material.

Herbs provided food for everyday cooking. Along with herbaceous plants containing certain properties, they were used for medicinal purposes, for savoring or embellishing in cooking, and for making perfumes. In the Talmud various herbs are advocated as cosmetics. They were the principle source of remedies in ancient times. Some were valued as cures. Others were regarded as protection against various illnesses. In the Bible "balm" is defined as effective in easing pain (Jer. 8:22, 51:8). Toxic herbs from which poisons are extracted, such as "gall," "hemlock," and "wormwood," are also mentioned in the Bible. These were administered in extremely small doses for ailments, as stated by Greek and Roman medical writers.

Spices extracted from certain aromatic vegetable substances were esteemed for cosmetics, perfumes, incense, sacred oils, and burial preparations. The Bible cites that the women brought "spices and ointment" to the sepulcher of Jesus (Luke 23:55-24:1). Utilized for compounding ointments and cosmetics were spices such as aloes, cassia, spikenard, and saffron. Importation of such precious spices was fabulously expensive.

Annual and biennial herbs and spices are best purchased from companies specializing in seeds or from firms offering young seedlings each season. Unless you raise the perennials from seeds, they must come from companies dealing in plants.

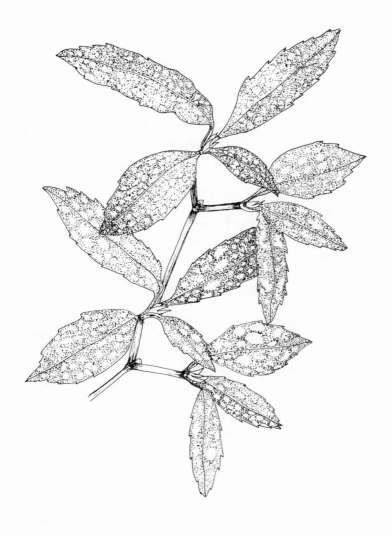

ALOE

Aloe succotrina
Biblical term: Aloes

THE NEW TESTAMENT "ALOES" is the true and bitter *Aloe succotrina* indigenous to steep cliffs and rocky slopes of Cape Province, South Africa. It is a succulent herb of the lily family with thick fleshy leaves. From the leaves is expressed a pale honey-colored sap, which is collected and evaporated. The active principles, termed "aloins," are extracted by water, and in Jesus' day sweet-smelling spices were added to make a precious anointing oil for use in embalming (John 19:39). Anointing oil was in constant demand throughout the Near East, not only to purify bodies of the dead, but also for its use in religious rites. Aloes and spices of great worth had to be imported from distant lands, rendering them extremely costly (Mark 14:4–5). They were kept in small vessels with narrow openings, from which they were poured carefully, drop by drop (Matthew 26:7). Sap from the leaves of the plant was also condensed and employed as a bitter-tasting purgative.

A. *succotrina* is found in small to large groups, growing up to 4 feet in height. The leaves are long and sword shaped, branched and re-branched into closely packed rosettes. Margins of the dull, grayish green to green leaves have whitish, hard, and sinewy borders, armed on the edges with firm, white teeth. When cut the leaf edges turn purplish. The young plants are stemless, but older ones usually have stems and are clothed with the residue of dried leaves. Dazzling, glossy, red or scarlet flowers bloom on a stalk in dense and tubular clusters during late summer.

Most important factors in successfully growing *A. succotrina* are excellent drainage, a rich, peaty, acid soil, a frost-free situation, and a place sheltered from the hot, drying rays of the afternoon sun. It shows to best advantage standing alone as a single specimen or grown beneath shrubs and trees requiring the same type of soil. It does not grow well in summer-rainfall areas, but if started from seed, it will usually adapt to adverse conditions. As with other aloes, *A. succotrina* may be propagated by detaching offsets from the parent plant.

Aloes are easily grown indoors, although there they rarely produce flowers. The soil must always be allowed to dry out between water-

Nicodemus . . . brought a mixture of myrrh and aloes, about an hundred pound weight.
(John 19:39)

ings to prevent the roots from rotting. Favoring high humidity, they should be misted frequently. A liquid fertilizer applied while they are in active growth helps to keep them healthy.

CAMOMILE, CHAMOMILE

Anthemis chia
Biblical reference: "clothe the grass"

A COMMON HERB THAT OCCURS IN great abundance in untilled soil and on dry, stony hillsides of Palestine is the small camomile, *Anthemis chia*. This is a spreading annual, with dainty, white, daisylike flowers blooming on long stalks from January until May. Growing amidst the grass, they are a beautiful sight to behold. But like the grass, the camomile appears for only a few weeks and soon withers after the rains cease. Camomile and grass, upon drying, are gathered up and destroyed. Some authorities believe Jesus referred to this wildflower when he rebuked the disciples for the fears they had concerning sufficient clothing as they continued to follow Him. Just as God takes care of the plants, so should the disciples have faith in the Father's promise to supply all needs, Jesus explained (Luke 12:28).

The lacy, light green, finely cut leaves send forth a strong, aromatic scent, especially when bruised. Ancient Egyptians used the dried leaves steeped in wine to reduce high fevers. The flower heads with golden-yellow, buttonlike centers yield a fragrant but bitter volatile oil. More familiar to us is the similar low-growing Roman camomile, *A. nobilis,* a creeping hardy perennial native to southern Europe. In the past English gardeners used this camomile as a ground cover. The flower stalks grow to a height of 3 to 12 inches, which, when cut release the fruity smell of ripe apples. A delightful and refreshing tea is made from the dried flower heads and consumed to induce a soothing, sedative effect. Camomile tea is sometimes brewed from both flowers and leaves or blended with other herbs. The leaves are made into a poultice to heal burns and cuts.

Roman camomile will grow in any ordinary well-drained soil and favors a sunny location. Young plants will spread over the ground and remain green most of the year. After the first year, they tolerate the driest of conditions. The flower heads begin to show in late May and continue to appear over a long period. They·are harvested when in full bloom and dried on a screen. Propagation is from seed, by division of roots in spring or fall, or from cuttings.

This fine little herb is superb for edgings or groupings on the edge of borders, as a lawn substitute, or between steppingstones. It grows well indoors as an annual, from seed sown at any time, but to produce flowers, the plant must be kept under fluorescent light.

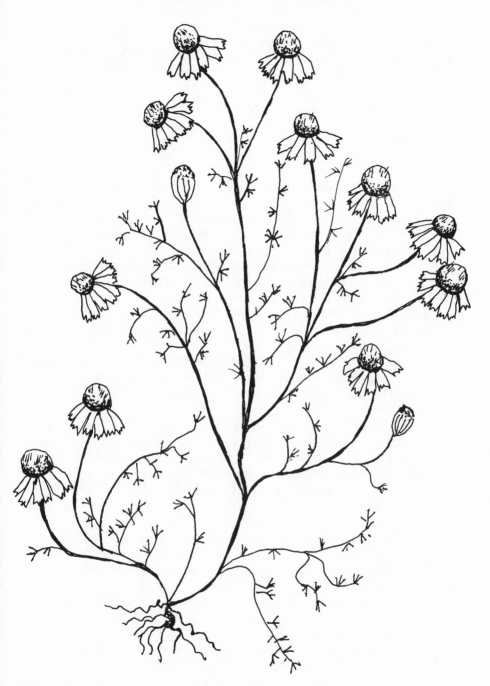

If then God so clothe the grass, which is to day in the field,
and tomorrow is cast in the oven.
(Luke 12:28)

CHARLOCK, WILD MUSTARD

Brassica arvensis
Biblical term: Nettles

CHARLOCK IS CONSIDERED A DETRIMENTAL weed prone to invade cultivated land and waste places, especially in the small grainfields of
Palestine. Many botanists think it was present in biblical times. Wherever the little yellow-flowered herb becomes established, it spreads
by seed faster than the grain plants. Soon its heavy foliage smothers
out the crop. Solomon, in the poetic parable of the sluggard (Proverbs 24:30–34), strides through the neglected fields of an indolent
man, observes the thorny bushes, the overgrown charlock, and the
stone wall guarding the property sorely in need of repair. The wise
ruler adeptly warns: shirking agricultural tasks will bring poverty and
ruin to a farmer.

In many sections of the United States, charlock is now a naturalized
pest, appearing in alfalfa, barley, oat, rye, and wheat fields. Farmers
must be forever alert to control it, not only to remove the culprit but
to destroy it by fire.

Charlock is an annual mustardlike herb 1 to 3 feet tall, branched
near the top with a few bristly hairs. The lower leaves are hairy and
coarsely toothed, the upper ones becoming progressively smaller. At
the ends of the branches are clusters of flowers, each bearing four
bright yellow petals. Long seed pods with stout conical beaks dis-
perse globular black or dark purplish-brown seeds from May to September. These are known to live in the soil for many years.

The young leaves of charlock are eaten as salad greens together
with cress, endive, or lettuce, or combined with cream cheese in sandwiches. Sometimes the green tops are cooked as a vegetable. The
plant, being closely related to the cabbage, has rather sharp and
strong-tasting foliage. As a vigorous and rampant weed, it should be
grown in a garden with great care in order to prevent a widespread
invasion. This can be done by destroying all seed pods, except for
seeds reserved for planting. Seeds can be sown in a container during
winter and placed by a sunny window, and the leaves may be cut when
needed for salads and garnishings.

And, lo, it was all grown over with thorns,
and nettles had covered the face thereof.
                              (Proverbs 24:31)

CORIANDER

Coriandrum sativum
Biblical term: Coriander

WHILE THE ISRAELITES JOURNEYED through the rugged terrain of the Sinai peninsula, God provided a welcome sweet-flavored supplement to their diet in the form of honeydew manna, which was compared with coriander seed in color, size, and taste (Exodus 16:31; Numbers 7–8). Coriander grows wild in Egypt and has been cultivated for thousands of years in Palestine. Seeds of the plant were discovered as funeral offerings in Egyptian tombs, and mention of coriander is made in a papyrus found in the tomb of Cheops near Cairo, leaving no doubt that coriander was familiar to the Israelites before the Exodus. People of those days valued the aromatic, spicy, oil-containing seeds as a seasoning and for their medicinal properties. Early Romans spread coriander and cumin seeds over meat to keep it from spoiling. The aromatic leaves, picked when young, are regarded by Egyptians as a delightful addition to salads and soups.

Common coriander, *Coriandrum sativum,* is an annual herb growing to about 12 inches in height. It has dark green, finely divided, fern-like foliage, the lower leaves broadly lobed. It develops tiny, white or pinkish-white, flat clusters of flowers about eight weeks after planting, which are followed three weeks later by maturing globular, scented, grayish-white seeds. When the seed heads turn brown, they are ready to be clipped off and dried in an airy place. The capsules are then removed and the seeds dried on trays in a warm room, where their pleasant fragrance becomes more distinct. If stored in tightly covered containers, their flavor improves with age. Coriander seeds eaten whole, ground, or crushed have a sweet, delicate taste, described by some as that of a combination of lemon peel and sage.

Modern cooks use the dried seeds to impart savor to beans, beef stews, poultry stuffings, and curry dishes. The ground seeds go into breads, cakes, cookies, and confectioneries. They may be sprinkled over cottage cheese, stewed fruits, fruit salads, and soups. Young leaves of coriander are often chopped into salads, sauces, and steaks for a change of flavor. The seeds are used in the commercial production of curry powder, frankfurters, and other processed meats. And they are used in medicine to disguise the unpleasant taste of some drugs.

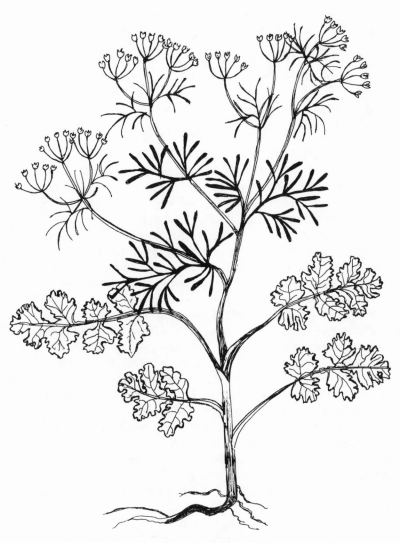

Manna . . . was like coriander seed; white: and the taste of it was like wafers made with honey.
(Exodus 16:31)

Any fairly rich, well-drained garden soil will suit coriander, but full sun and regular waterings are needed for good growth. The seeds are sown after danger of frost has passed in the place where the plants are to grow, because they do not flourish in cold weather nor do they transplant well. Due to their fast growth, successive plantings are advisable. Coriander can be brought to maturity in a pot if exposed to direct sunlight.

FENNEL-FLOWER, NUTMEG-FLOWER

Nigella sativa
Biblical term: Fitches

"FITCHES" IN ISAIAH'S PARABLE (28:23–29) is identified as fennel or nutmeg-flower, *Nigella sativa,* an aromatic herb long cultivated in Bible lands for its tiny, hot-tasting, black seeds. They are an Eastern substitute for black pepper and are still used as a condiment for seasoning cakes and breads, particularly to sprinkle on the tops of bread loaves to enrich the flavor. In the quoted passage, Isaiah described the farmer's systematic way of preparing the ground before sowing the seeds, and then of broadcasting the cumin and fennel seeds, giving greater care in sowing the more valuable crops such as wheat, barley, and spelt. The farmer's orderly working schedule, learned from God, is likened to God's steadfast plan to sustain His people, even in view of the ultimate destruction facing the Northern Kingdom.

Fennel-flower, a relative of the familiar love-in-a-mist, *Nigella damascena,* is a branching, foot-tall plant, frequently found naturalized in fields and waste places of Mediterranean regions. It has bright green, finely dissected, lacelike foliage and light blue or whitish solitary blossoms produced at the ends of the stems. Each buttercuplike flower is surrounded by a green, many-branched, lacy crown growing from its base. The fruit is an inflated, five-chambered capsule, containing many hard black seeds. Farmers in Isaiah's day beat the capsules with a rod to release the seeds. Isaiah's allusion to the method of harvesting the seeds was meant as a forewarning that God would employ foreign powers as a rod to discipline Israel.

Seeds of fennel-flower hold a spicy, pungent oil known to increase the flow of saliva and to stimulate the appetite. Moslem women ate them mixed with a conserve to obtain obesity. Herb gardeners today use the seeds to enhance curries, sauces, and soups, or in any dish requiring black pepper. The interesting seed capsules are highly decorative in dried arrangements, while the fresh material adds airiness in a bouquet.

Fennel-flower is not particular about soil and withstands considerable drought, but it needs full sun. Seeds sown in the spring come quickly into bloom, but dry up in summer. The plants soon reseed themselves by dispersing seeds through openings at the top of the capsules. When sown in beds or borders among established plants, they call for little attention except thinning out to 8 inches apart.

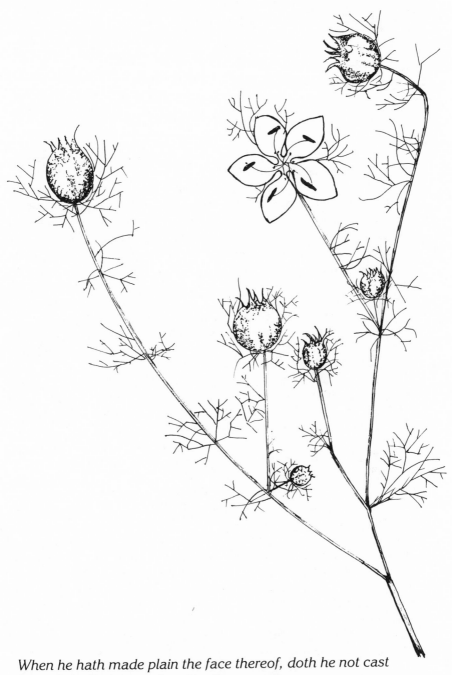

*When he hath made plain the face thereof, doth he not cast
abroad the fitches, and scatter the cummin.*
(Isaiah 28:25)

FERULA

Ferula galbaniflua
Biblical term: Galbanum

ONE OF THE ELABORATE FURNISHINGS of the portable tentlike Tabernacle built under the direction of Moses was the golden altar of incense,
upon which burned daily a combination of aromatic substances reserved for the worship of God (Exodus 30:34–38). Among the constit-
uents of the holy incense was galbanum, an imported gum resin. It
was extracted from the plant called ferula, *Ferula galbaniflua,* indigenous from Syria to Persia. Stems of this plant exude a milklike juice
that hardens into light brown or yellowish lumps on contact with air.
When the resin was mixed with the fragrant spices and burned, the
offensive musky odor was absorbed. The result was a pleasant aroma
and a longer lasting material. A substance obtained from Syrian ferula is employed as a remedy for convulsions. It is also used in the
manufacture of lacquer. Although six species of ferula grow wild in
Israel, their resins are not utilized.

Ferula is a robust, strong rooted, herbaceous plant, the erect flowering stems reaching several feet in height. A perennial, it is found on
dry hills, on limestone, and on stony slopes. Its large, dark green,
feathery leaves are many times divided into fine segments, borne on
stout, hollow stems. The leaves die down in summer to reappear in
the fall. The numerous yellow flowers, equipped with resin canals, are
arranged in flat, umbrella-shaped heads on stalks rising from the
main stem. Pith in the dry stems burns slowly and has been used as
tinder since early times. In some parts of the Mediterranean the stems
are utilized to construct furniture.

The giant fennel, *F. communis,* is similar to ferula and is frequently
grown in American gardens for its beautiful carrotlike foliage and
large clusters of small golden flowers. It is a hardy perennial herb of
Mediterranean origin, growing 8 to 12 feet tall. In spring it presents a
magnificent show of blossoms on tall stems. The plant is easily propagated by division.

Any good well-drained soil is satisfactory for either ferula or giant
fennel. Given a position in direct sunlight, both species will withstand
hot winds and drought. Planted in an open spot in an informal perennial hedge or grown in a container, they offer a striking display of
beauty.

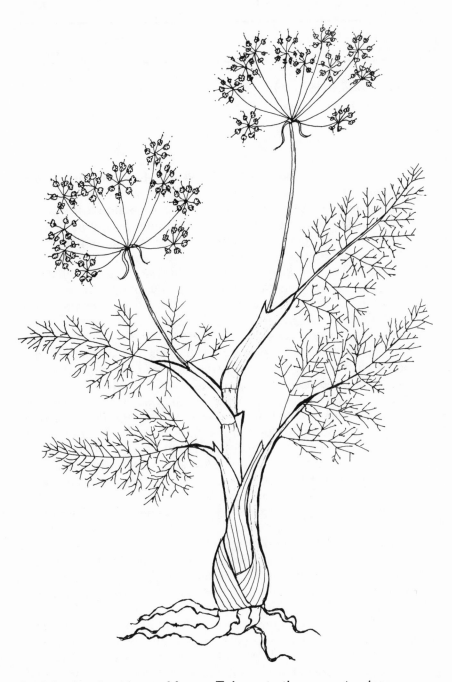

And the Lord said unto Moses, Take unto thee sweet spices,
stacte, and onycha, and galbanum.
(Exodus 30:34)

FLAX

Linum usitatissimum
Biblical term: Flax

FLAX WAS CULTIVATED IN PREHISTORIC TIMES, probably originating in the Mediterranean region. Early Egyptians grew it (Exodus 9:31), and Palestinian women were praised for their contribution to the production of linen (Proverbs 31:13). Flax is a winter annual in warm climates, where it ripens about five months after planting. In biblical times, the stalks were pulled up by the roots when the plants had developed flower heads, and were laid on the flat rooftops to dry in the sun (Joshua 2:6). Then the stalks were partly rotted in water for several weeks to loosen the fibers from the soft tissues. The fibers were dried and bleached, then separated by washing and combing. Finally they were spun and woven into cloth (Proverbs 31:19).

In ancient Palestine, spinning the threads and weaving them on looms was mainly a home industry performed by women who also sold the finished cloth to merchants (Proverbs 31:24). Various grades of material were woven. The finest quality was made into garments for rulers (Genesis 41:42) and the wealthy (Luke 16:19), for hangings in the Tabernacle (Exodus 25:4), and for the sails of Tyrian trading vessels (Ezekiel 27:7). Coarse but durable linen fabrics furnished clothing for the poor. From this oldest known textile fiber was made the fabric in which the body of the crucified Jesus was wound, along with a mixture of spices (John 19:40).

Cultivated flax, *L. usitatissimum,* is a slender herb about 3 feet high, with lance-shaped leaves, branching stems, and sky-blue flowers. The flowers turn into small, dry pods holding shiny, flat, brown seeds. Oil produced from the seeds is used chiefly in the manufacture of linseed oil, which is combined in paints and varnishes and in making linoleum and printer's ink. Flax seed is widely used in medicines and in herb teas.

Flax is hardy and grows successfully in all parts of the United States. Its pretty, shallow-cupped, five-petaled flowers bloom abundantly from late spring into summer and fall. It is drought resistant, enjoying full sunlight and a well-drained soil. The plants grow easily from seed sown where they are to remain. They are delightful in rock gardens and as group plantings among other herbs and will naturalize freely in waste places.

*She seeketh wool, and flax, and worketh
willingly with her hands.*
(Proverbs 31:13)

LADY'S THISTLE, MILK THISTLE

Silybum marianum
Biblical term: Thistle

MORE THAN ONE HUNDRED KINDS OF thistles thrive in the Mediterranean region, mostly in neglected fields and wild places. The seeds, over-topped by tufts of silky hairs, are scattered far and wide by the wind. Despite the fact that some thistles attain great beauty, they all find disfavor for their ability to multiply rapidly, and their vigorous roots make them difficult to eradicate. Among the numerous species found in the Holy Land is the lady's or milk thistle, *Silybum marianum*. The large prickly leaves and veins at its base are marbled with white, traditionally explained as being splashes of Mary's milk. This is the thistle associated with the prophecy of Hosea (10:8) and Genesis 3:17–18.

In Hosea's day, the hilly town of Aven (Bethel) had become a center of idol worship, and the people of the northern kingdom had eagerly adopted the pagan creeds. The deep infiltration of idols into the sanc-tuaries, accompanied by moral decay, removed any vital relationship between the Israelites and God. Because of their unfaithfulness, the prophet foresaw certain exile of the people, their once cultivated fields and lands turned into a wilderness. A visible sign of desolation and ruin would be the thorns and thistles overgrowing the sites of the Israelites' former homes.

The handsome lady's thistle is a robust annual or biennial herb, growing to 4 feet or more in height. The glossy, deeply lobed leaves have wavy, spiny edged margins and prominent veins on the under-sides. Surrounding the large, solitary, purplish-red disk flowers are numerous curved spine-tipped bracts. Straw-colored down tips the dry seeds. A most aggressive plant, it is now naturalized throughout California.

Lady's thistle was once grown extensively for food and as an ingre-dient in herbal remedies. The long taproots were boiled and placed in soups and stews, the flower heads were eaten like artichokes, and the leaves and stout young stems were used in salads. Even today the fresh young leaves are enjoyed in salads by the Arabs.

The plant may be grown in the garden or in tubs, either as an orna-

. . . the thorn and the thistle shall come up on their altars;
and they shall say to the mountains, Cover us;
and to the hills, Fall on us.
(Hosea 10:8)

mental plant or an edible vegetable. The fresh or dried heads provide
excellent material for flower arrangements. Propagation is by seeds
sown in any ordinary garden soil in full sun and in the place where the
plant is to mature. Lady's thistle will blossom the first year if planted
early in the spring.

MANDRAKE

Mandragora officinarum
Biblical term: Mandrakes

THE TRUE MANDRAKE IS A PERENNIAL herb belonging to the potato family and a native of the Mediterranean region. It is commonly found throughout the Holy Land in stony places and deserted fields. Because the thick root divides into two leglike forked branches somewhat resembling the lower limbs of a human, countless superstitions became associated with the plant. Ancient Canaanites ascribed magical powers to the roots, using them extensively in their fertility rituals. In some parts of the Near East, women still think the presence of mandrake in their homes will induce pregnancy and stimulate passion. The juicy, pulpy fruit, long known to contain poisonous properties, is considered not only a delicacy but also a love potion. It ripens all through the Holy Land during the wheat harvest, and Rachel, the childless wife of Jacob, presumably wanted her sister's mandrakes to cure her barrenness (Genesis 30:1–15).

Mandrake, also called love apple, is a beautiful plant, with dark green, broad, lance-shaped leaves reaching to about a foot in height. Wrinkled and wavy margined, they grow directly from a long, tuberous taproot and spread out in a circle close to the soil. Arising from the center of the leaves are short-stalked, cup-shaped flowers, borne in clusters and purple in color. The plum sized, sweet fruit, ranging from yellow to orange, is pleasantly scented (Song of Solomon 7:13). Through the ages, mandrake has been used as a narcotic to dull pain and induce sleep. It was employed as an anesthetic in surgical operations before the discovery of ether.

This herb, credited with the greatest of magical powers and once highly regarded in medicine, is a rarity in American gardens. If plants or seeds can be obtained, mandrake would be a permanent source of interest and admiration. It grows best in full sun or under the light shade of deciduous trees, requiring little attention. Like most herbs, it prefers a nonacid, well-drained soil. The plant should be watered in periods when rainfall is inadequate.

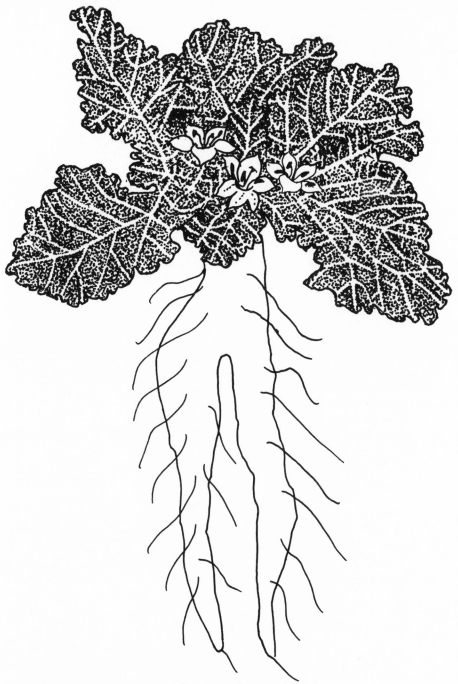

*Then Rachel said to Leah, Give me, I pray thee,
of thy son's mandrakes.*
(Genesis 30:14)

MARJORAM

Origanum syriacum
Biblical term: Hyssop

MODERN SCHOLARS HAVE PRETTY WELL identified the hyssop of the Old Testament as the Syrian marjoram, *Origanum maru* or *syriacum,* a member of the mint family common in Palestine and found growing in dry places, among rocks, and in crevices in walls. When it grows under such unfavorable conditions, this rather bushy herb attains only a few inches in height. These facts are in accord with the passage which relates to Solomon's ability to discuss with authority all matters pertaining to plant life (I Kings 4:33).

On the other hand, under suitable conditions Syrian marjoram attains a height of 1 to 3 feet. Its erect, stiff branches and thick, broad, oval leaves are hairy, while the small, whitish flowers form rounded clusters at the ends of the branches. The children of Israel used the branches as a brush to sprinkle blood on lintels and doorposts upon the night of their departure from Egypt (Exodus 12:21–22). In time, this herb came to be a symbol of purification (Psalms 51:7).

None of the Palestinian species of marjoram is available to us, but wild marjoram, *O. vulgare,* our only cultivated species, is quite similar in structure. It is a 2 foot tall, sweetly scented, aromatic herb, carrying in midsummer rounded clusters of tiny, purplish-pink or white blossoms. Its leaves are a dull gray green with purple stems. Herbalists of old recommended it for rheumatic swellings, toothache, boils, and sore throat. The fresh or dried leaves are especially popular in Italian and Spanish cookery. They give a distinctive hot and pungent flavor to spaghetti sauces, soups, salads, and all meat dishes. The fresh flowers serve well in summer arrangements and when dried for winter bouquets or wreaths.

Perennial wild marjoram needs a sunny location and a well-drained, moderately rich garden soil kept on the dry side. The foliage must be trimmed frequently to prevent blossoming. To have marjoram for the winter months in colder climates, pot up a few plants in the fall and place them indoors by a sunny window. (The green leaves produce considerably more flavor than do the dried ones). Propagation is by seeds after danger of frost is past, division of the underground stems in spring, or by rooting cuttings. Plants three years old or more should be discarded.

And he spake of trees, from the cedar tree that is in Lebanon even unto the hyssop that springeth out of the wall.
(I Kings 4:33)

Planted at the edge of a border or along a path, the little bushes will thicken quickly. It would be interesting to insert small marjoram plants into crevices of a low rock wall, pressing sphagnum moss and soil around the roots of each plant. Keep the plants well watered until established. They will soon represent an attractive remembrance of the biblical verse.

MUSTARD

Brassica nigra
Biblical term: Mustard

SEVERAL KINDS OF WILD MUSTARD ABOUND in the Holy Land, the black mustard being the one commonly cultivated for its aromatic seed and oil. In rich soil, this annual plant reaches treelike proportions, measuring 10 to 15 feet in height, with a central stem sometimes attaining the thickness of a man's arm. The stem and branches harden in the fall and become firm enough to harbor small birds that feast on the seeds. Black mustard is a familiar sight along the shores of the Sea of Galilee, where Jesus spoke to the multitudes on the subject of the Kingdom of God. Jesus, in a parable (Luke 13:19), compares the fast growth of the Gospel message to the rapid development of this minute mustard seed into a treelike plant. Although not a tree in the scientific sense, it is in accord with the Oriental concept of such an exceptional plant.

In the Near East, the brownish-black mustard seeds were ground into powder to provide fragrance and a strong but pleasant taste to food and medicine. Oil from the seeds was used for lighting. The stiff, hairy, dark green foliage was cooked as a vegetable and used for fodder. Rising from a leafy stem, clusters of lemon-yellow flowers terminate at the top and side branches of the plant. Later, inch-long seed pods hug the stem. The tiny seeds can survive burial for many years and will start to grow when brought to the surface of the soil.

Today the seeds of the black mustard are the chief source of commercial mustards. Growing 4 to 6 feet tall, the plant is cultivated in home gardens primarily for its wealth of succulent leaves. Mustard greens have high nutritional value, being rich in minerals and vitamins. Seed plantings should be scheduled for the cooler months of the season, winter in the south, early spring and fall in northern climates. To prevent plants from going to seed, pick off the flower heads as soon as they appear. These may be used to add flavor and color to salads. Pick the outer leaves as they develop, or pull the entire plant at the peak of its growth.

Mustard requires a medium-rich soil, full sun, and regular waterings. To help keep the soil cool and moist, mulch it after the plants are about 4 inches tall. Mustard may be grown in flower pots under artificial light, at a room temperature under 70 degrees F.

It is like a grain of mustard seed, which a man took, and cast into his garden; and it grew, and waxed a great tree.

(Luke 13:19)

RESURRECTION PLANT

Anastatica hierochuntica
Biblical reference: "rolling thing"

ISAIAH, IN A PROPHETIC SOLILOQUY, saw the hostile armies bent on destroying Jerusalem making a sudden and hasty retreat (II Kings 19:34–36) and compared the fleeing host to the resurrection plant, *Anastatica hierochuntica,* driven before a wind storm. The plant he alluded to grows in abundance around Jericho, throughout Syria, and on the deserts of Asia Minor. It is a fernlike herb of the mustard family seldom more than a foot across when expanded, at which time it reveals small, toothed leaves and minute white flowers. After the seeds have ripened the slender branches become dry and curve inward, giving the plant a ball-like structure. The force of the wind breaks the stem loose at the ground line and sends the plant spinning like a "wheel" (Psalms 83:13) across the flat expanses of sand, scattering its seeds along the way. Often hundreds of resurrection plants pile up in a heap, only to be again tossed about by strong winds.

This little desert plant has the remarkable ability to unfold its branches during the rainy season or upon settling in a moist spot. It then turns from an apparently lifeless object into a living plant bearing roots, although it may have rested for several years in its dry state. From this capacity to renew its life it has received its common name, and many visitors to the Holy Land treasure the plant as a souvenir.

An herb sold in the United States under the name of resurrection plant, *Selaginella lepidophylla,* is native to deserts from Texas to South America. A perennial growing to 4 inches high, it has the same characteristics as the one of the Isaiah passage. In damp soil or in a dish of water, its fernlike leaves slowly unfold and become a lush green. If the plant is allowed to dry out, the color gradually fades until the plant appears to be dead. It thrives indoors or out, with or without sun. It may be propagated from seed and from pieces of the plant inserted in water or in a pot filled with moist soil.

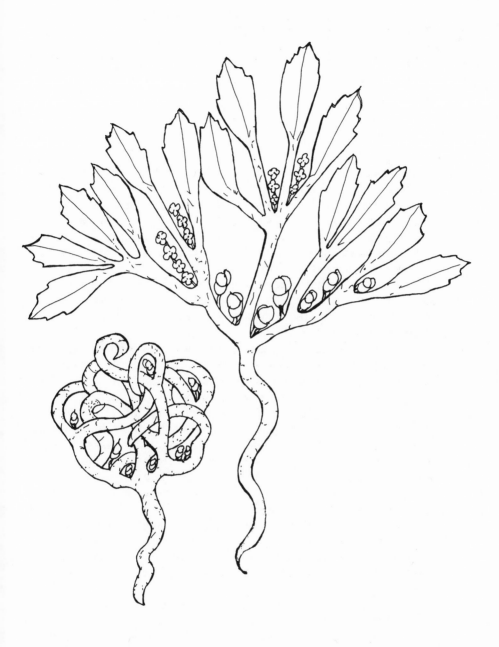

*God shall rebuke them, and they shall flee far off, and shall
be chased as the chaff of the mountains before the wind,
and like a rolling thing before the whirlwind.*

(Isaiah 17:13)

SAFFRON CROCUS

Crocus sativus
Biblical term: Saffron

IN THE POETIC VERSE from Song of Solomon (4:14), the shepherd lover of the beautiful country girl of Shulen expresses his constant love and rapturous admiration. He compares her winsomeness to an enchanting enclosed garden filled with exotic fragrant spices. The saffron he includes is usually interpreted as the fall-blooming crocus, *Crocus sativus,* known and valued for centuries. It is believed to be identical with the heavily scented saffron grown in Solomon's extensive walled gardens, for it is a native of Asia Minor and the eastern Mediterranean lands. Egyptians strewed their palace floors with the flowers. The saffron obtained from the herb was extremely expensive, being symbolic of kings and wealth.

The saffron crocus has grassy basal leaves 4 to 6 inches long. These appear at the same time as the stemless lilac or purple flowers. Produced from the large golden stigmas is the famous yellow saffron dye so widely used in coloring and flavoring food. As soon as a flower opens it is picked by hand. The three aromatic stigmas are removed and set out to dry in the sun. More than seventy thousand blossoms are needed to yield a single pound of the precious spice. Fortunately, a little saffron goes a long way in a beverage to give it a subtle taste or to add a rich golden color to rice, cheese, and baked goods. Formerly, the stigmas and upper part of the style were used for dyeing cloth yellow. In England during the Middle Ages much saffron was grown to provide the basic material for saffron tea cakes. It is an essential ingredient in making *arroz con polo,* the world-renowned rice and chicken dish of Spanish origin. The dried stigmas are employed commercially in eastern Europe in manufacturing perfumes and medicines.

Corms of the saffron crocus are planted in August for flowers in October. Set the small corms 2 to 3 inches deep in light, porous soil in a sunny location. Seedlings coming up around the plants will soon increase the supply. When the plants become crowded in 3 to 4 years, they should be dug up and respaced to about 6 inches apart. Stigmas harvested for future use are best stored in tight-lidded bottles.

As fall advances the satiny flower cups put on a splendid display in rock gardens, between steppingstones, massed in a bed, or in a warm

*Spikenard and saffron; calamus and cinnamon,
with all trees of frankincense.*
(Song of Solomon 4:14)

pocket next to the house. In places where there will be no mowing or cultivating, they are charming if naturalized in grass. Indoors a flash of color is obtained by growing the corms in a shallow pot or bowl set in a sunny window area.

SAGE

Salvia judaica
Biblical term: Candlestick

ONE OF THE FURNISHINGS IN THE TABERNACLE was a seven-branched candlestick made of pure gold. Thought to have been about five feet high, it consisted of a central shaft with three branches on each side. It was filled with pure olive oil and kept burning continuously outside the veil. Only the most skilled of craftsmen were entrusted with the making of the sacred object. Inspired by the blossoms of the sage plant which grows wild on the hills and mountains of Palestine, the shaft and branches took the shape of the pressed-out flower head. On each branch of the plant are whorls of buds, motivating the design for the globular ornaments of the candlestick. The most authentic example of the seven-branched candlestick is depicted on the marble Arch of Titus in Rome.

The Judean sage of the Bible is not obtainable in the United States, but the closely related common garden sage, *S. officinalis,* is our most widely cultivated herb. Of Mediterranean origin, it has been grown in gardens since the beginning of recorded history. Its Latin name, *Salvia,* meaning to save or heal, refers to the aromatic and fragrant oil extracted from the leaves. Physicians in the past recommended its strong tonic effects as a cure for almost every conceivable ailment. A hot drink made from the leaves is still reputed to relieve a common cold and digestive complaints. Through the years the aromatic fresh or dried leaves have retained popularity as a seasoning for stuffings, poultry dishes, roasts, and cheese. Fresh young leaves are used in salads and as a dentifrice to whiten teeth.

Garden sage is a shrubby perennial growing 8 to 30 inches in height, with a whitish, woolly stem and wrinkled, thick, lance-shaped, gray-green leaves. In late June or early July it produces terminal spikes of two-lipped, tubular, violet-blue flowers in whorls. The leaves and flowering tops are gathered and thoroughly dried away from the sun, then rubbed down for storing. Two cuttings in a season are possible from an established plant.

Sage likes a sunny site and a good, well-drained garden soil. It will grow for many years in the same location and is fairly drought resistant. New plants can be raised from seed sown in April, requiring two seasons to reach a usable size. Sage may also be propagated in the spring or fall by dividing old plants, by cuttings, or by layering.

*And he made the candlestick of pure gold: of beaten work
made he the candlestick; his shaft and his branch, his bowls,
his knops, and his flowers were of the same.*
(Exodus 37:17)

With its frosty gray foliage, garden sage gives special drama to a
rock garden or is effective as an accent plant among green foliaged
herbs. It is easily grown indoors in a pot if exposed to plenty of sun,
fresh air, and an evenly moist soil. When cut, the fragrant blooms and
striking leaves blend well with other flowers.

SALTWORT, SEA PURSLANE

Atriplex halimus
Biblical term: Mallows

JOB, WHILE AN OBJECT OF CONTEMPT AND persecution by youths who belonged to the lowest of social classes, recalled that the poor were grateful to gather the twigs and thick, leathery leaves of the "mallows" for food (Job 30:4). Mallows have been identified as saltwort or sea purslane, *Atriplex halimus*, a perennial herb whose taste and tolerance of seashore conditions has earned them their common names. This shrubby plant grows plentifully along the shores of the Mediterranean, on salt-rich inland sands of the Holy Land, and in the region of the Dead Sea. In biblical times saltwort was considered famine fare, and it is still eaten by the poor of the Near East. Sometimes the leaves are pickled and consumed as a relish.

This erect, many-branched, strong-growing shrub attains a height of 1 to 3 feet. The silvery-white evergreen leaves are oval or angular in shape. In late summer, clusters of yellowish flowers bloom on the ends of long, branched spikes. The leaves must be picked while young if they are to be used as food, because they become stringy and tough with age.

In the western part of the United States, native shrubs of the genus *Atriplex* are called saltbush. They thrive in alkaline desert soils or in direct seashore situations, making them similar to the mallows mentioned in Job. Many species are cultivated for their drought tolerance, fire resistance, and as erosion control on arid hillsides. Brewer saltbush, *A. breweri,* is similar to saltwort in appearance, with almost evergreen silvery-gray, oval or oblong leaves. Growing 5 to 7 feet in height and densely branched, it will form an attractive hedge or windbreak if plants are set 4 to 6 feet apart.

Outside their native habitat, saltwort or saltbush must have extremely fast soil drainage. Heavy applications of water should be limited to the blooming period, which occurs from February to May. They are raised best from seed, because they develop deep taproots and are not easily transplanted.

Who cut up mallows by the bushes,
and juniper roots for their meat.
(Job 30:4)

SPIKENARD

Nardostachys var. *Valeriana jatamansi*
Biblical term: Spikenard

IN THE TIME OF JESUS, ANOINTING the feet, head, or body of a guest was a sign of hospitality. The setting of the lovely story of Mary of Bethany honoring Jesus with the precious oil of spikenard was a supper of fellowship (Mark 14:3–8; John 12:1–7). After the seal of a narrow-necked alabaster flask was broken, the exquisite fragrance of the ointment filled the house. This exotic species of spikenard (Song of Solomon 1:12; 4:13, 14) comes from the cold, high pastures of Nepal, Tibet, and other regions of the Himalayas. An aromatic, reddish-colored liquid is extracted from the roots and young woolly stems. The ointment was treasured by the wealthy of Palestine, who used it principally in preparing bodies for burial. Conveyance of the product from remote India over difficult caravan routes caused it to be extremely expensive. So costly was Mary's gift of devotion that it represented the equivalent of a laborer's wage for the greater part of a year.

Spikenard, or nard, is a perennial herb of the Valerian family and related to the familiar *V. officinalis.* Its powerfully fragrant root, or rhizome, and young stems are still dried together for perfume making, especially in India. People of Eastern countries use the extract to scent clothing and tobacco. The odor is regarded as disagreeable by Western standards.

The easily acquired valerian of European origin is quite similar with its pointed lance-shaped leaves and sweet smelling, pale pink flowers growing in dense, flattened clusters at the ends of 3 to 5 foot tall branches. A volatile oil present in the thick rootstocks is used medically in an infusion, extract, or syrup as herbal remedies to promote sleep, soothe nerves, and treat epilepsy. Though the carrion aroma of the root is offensive to humans, it is appetizing to cats and has also been used as rat bait.

Valerian thrives in a fertile, moist garden soil, in sun or light shade. New plants are started from seed sown indoors in March and transplanted outdoors in mid-June. In fall or early spring, the spreading rootstocks of old plants may be divided.

Flowering from spring to early summer, valerian merges easily into a mixed herb garden or flower border. It is well suited for covering a bank, to use in small clumps, or singly as a tub subject. Scented like heliotrope, the cut flowers are splendid for bouquets.

Then took Mary a pound of ointment of spikenard,
very costly, and anointed the feet of Jesus.

(John 12:3)

WORMWOOD

Artemisia absinthium var. *judaica*
Biblical term: Wormwood

IN A SPECIAL PROPHESY OF JUDGMENT, Jeremiah risked his life to speak out against the false prophets of Jerusalem, courageously stating that not all who speak in God's name have been appointed to do so (Jeremiah 23:14–22). He refers to the bitter tasting wormwood, a symbol of bitter experience (Proverbs 5:4), to pronounce doom on the unscrupulous religious leaders of his day. Several species of wormwood grow on arid and uncultivated land in Palestine, North Africa, and Europe, all of which are aromatic, camphorous, and intensely bitter. *A. absinthium* and *A. judaica* are two species proposed by numerous authorities as the ones referred to in the Scriptures. The leaves and flowering stems of European wormwood *A. absinthium,* are compounded to produce a stimulating drink which not only produces inebriation but also contains poisonous narcotic properties. When taken consistently in large quantities it has a deteriorating effect on the nervous system and causes delirium, hallucinations, trembling, and even death (Lamentations 3:15, 19). Biblical references to this dangerous and most bitter of all herbs are usually associated with calamity and sorrow.

All wormwoods have much the same appearance. They are woody, shrublike, perennial herbs with silky, silvery-white foliage. The pungent, lacy leaves, like the chrysanthemum, are divided and cut. From midsummer until early fall, the 2 to 4 foot tall, many-branched plant bears, on long spikes, numerous small rounded yellow heads of fragrant flowers. European wormwood from ancient times was considered one of the most important of herbs because of its medicinal value. In the time of Dioscorides and Pliny it was employed as a cure for worms, hence the common name. A syrup or infusion was taken internally as a tonic, stimulant, and appetizer. Today the volatile oil of wormwood is used commercially in preparing liniments to apply to bruises, sprains, swellings, and lumbago. European wormwood is common along roadsides in the United States, where it has escaped cultivation.

Artemisias are welcomed in gardens, since their frosted color tones provide an interesting contrast to the prevailing greens. They give a definite accent in borders when planted among more brilliantly

Behold, I will feed them with wormwood,
and make them drink the water of gall.
                    (Jeremiah 23:15)

hued flowers and are attractive in containers. The blossoms and foliage make decorative floral combinations in bouquets. After the seed heads develop, the branches can be cut and dried to create winter arrangements such as everlasting wreaths and swags.

All that is required to grow wormwood is an ordinary garden soil, good drainage, and a dry, sunny location. Old plants tend to become woody and die out, so they should be renewed every three or four years during spring or fall. Plants may be started from seed, but are slow in germinating.

PART 4

Flowers of the Field and Garden

Flowers of the field are one of the outstanding features of Palestine, lending vibrant enchantment to the ordinarily drab and dry hillsides. No other place in the world supports such an enormous variety of wildflowers concentrated within a relatively small area. Soon after the rains of March and April, the countryside literally comes ablaze with color. Blooming in profusion, but not mentioned in the Bible, are the daisy, gladioli, iris, larkspur, marigold, jasmine, and squill. Especially prominent are flowers of the lily groups, which rise from bulbs that hibernate in dry periods until the rains and warmth of spring enable them to send up leaves, flowers, and seeds to broadcast. Within a month's time, burning hot days and scorching east winds destroy the multicolored vegetation. Other native flowers dwell wild and undisturbed in marshes and under the shade of woodland trees.

Few flowers were cultivated in biblical times purely for ornament. With the exception of kings and the wealthy, garden space was reserved for practical plants. The Song of Solomon has the longest list of garden flowers, although many are not given specific names. This has resulted in much debate over the true identity of numerous kinds, in particular the lilies. The following entries of individual flowers indicate what modern botanists believe to have been those represented in the Bible.

ANEMONE, WINDFLOWER

Anemone coronaria
Biblical term: Lilies

THE SINGLE-FLOWERED POPPY ANEMONE or windflower, *A. coronaria,* inhabits hills and mountainous slopes from Palestine to Spain in such places as olive groves and vineyards. During the season Jesus delivered the Sermon on the Mount, these harbingers of spring robed the hillsides in a dazzling array of color. Because of their vivacious blooms of scarlet, blue, or white, they are considered one of the most special sights of Palestine. A number of wildflowers have been suggested for the "lilies of the field," and it is probable that the Hebrew term embraces a wider scope than that of our modern lily. Therefore many scholars suggest that Jesus referred to the poppy anemone, because it is the most brilliant of all Palestinian wildflowers and seems ideally suited to Jesus' illustration. The discourse delivered to the disciples within the hearing of others depreciates the high value attached to worldly possessions, pointing out that not even the grandeur of Solomon's royal robes could match the natural beauty of the wildflowers (Matthew 6:28–34; Luke 12:27–32).

The poppy anemone is a tuberous-rooted perennial of the buttercup family which sends up long-stalked, vivid green, basal leaves that are deeply cut and lobed. Each stiff, 10 to 18 inch stalk produces a poppylike flower, often with differently colored centers. In temperate climates the plants will display a continuous show of blooms throughout spring, summer, and fall if there are successive plantings and if they are slightly shaded as the weather becomes warm.

Tubers of anemones must be planted in the fall to have a spritely show of flowers in early spring. New plants can be readily started from seed or by division of older tubers. In mild climate areas the tubers are set directly in the soil. Where winters are severe anemones are not dependably hardy and need protection indoors or in a greenhouse. Transplanted to the garden after the last frost, they will bloom in May and June. They thrive in sun or semishade and a well-drained, moderately rich soil and will multiply for years. *A. coronaria* has given rise to several horticultural varieties, including the single-flowered poppylike "De Cain" which comes in a mixture of gorgeous shades.

The poppy anemone is especially valued as a source of long-lasting cut flowers. In a garden it is highly decorative planted in naturalistic

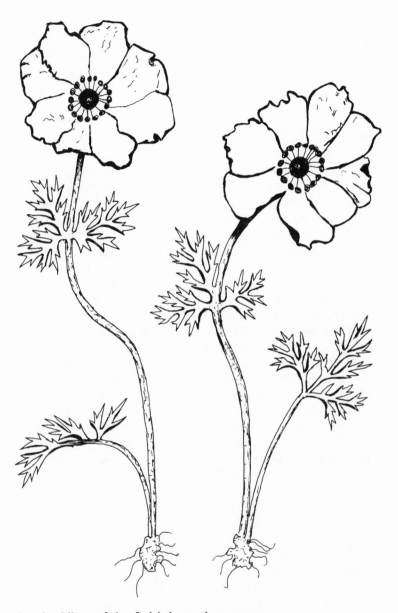

Consider the lillies of the field, how they grow;
they toil not, neither do they spin.
            (Matthew 6:28)

drifts, grouped in rockery pockets, or established in a border inter-
mingled with the biblical tulips and hyacinths. Plant 6 to 8 tubers in a
6 inch pot for large, showy flowers to brighten an indoor setting.

CYCLAMEN

Cyclamen persicum
Biblical term: Lilies

SOME SCHOLARS FEEL CERTAIN THAT the "lilies" to which Jesus referred (Matthew 6:28–30; Luke 12:27, 28) were the supremely attractive cyclamen, *C. persicum*. They grow in abundance on hills and mountainsides and in meadows from Greece to Palestine, on the edges of thickets, in rock fissures, and alongside old walls. During the spring season they capture the interest and admiration of all passersby with their breathtaking blossoms of pink, lilac, and white.

Cyclamens are low-growing perennials with large tuberous rootstocks. From the surface of the roots spring a number of long-stalked, heart-shaped, dark green basal leaves, often beautifully marked with silvery splashes. The sweetly scented flowers, blotched with dark purple at the throat, are borne on strong erect stems that stand well above the foliage. Their narrow lance-shaped petals turn upward, resembling shooting stars. In late fall and winter, seed capsules develop on twisted, pigtail stalks. Numerous variations have been developed by horticulturists from this wild species, including the large-flowered Persian cyclamen sold by florists for winter interior decoration. From late fall to spring they produce an abundance of flowers in many exquisite shades of pink and red.

Cyclamens benefit from a rich, porous soil with plenty of humus and moisture. Where grown outdoors, they require a well-shaded, sheltered location. Planted in naturalized clumps beneath mature trees and shrubs, they reseed themselves and multiply rapidly. A covering is needed in cold winter regions as a protection against freezing. Tubers are planted in the dormant period (June to August), with the upper half visible above the soil surface. Cyclamen grow readily from seed, taking 18 or more months to flower. After sowing, keep the plantings in complete darkness for 40 days.

The large-flowered *C. persicum* makes an unusually beautiful potted plant, indoors or out. Used as potted outdoor plants, they offer the advantage of their elegant seasonal colors but can be moved out of sight when the foliage dies back. When placed in an airy, cool, well-lighted indoor environment, the blooms will last much longer. Light should be indirect and the soil kept moist. After the flowers are gone and the foliage has dried, the tubers may be planted outdoors.

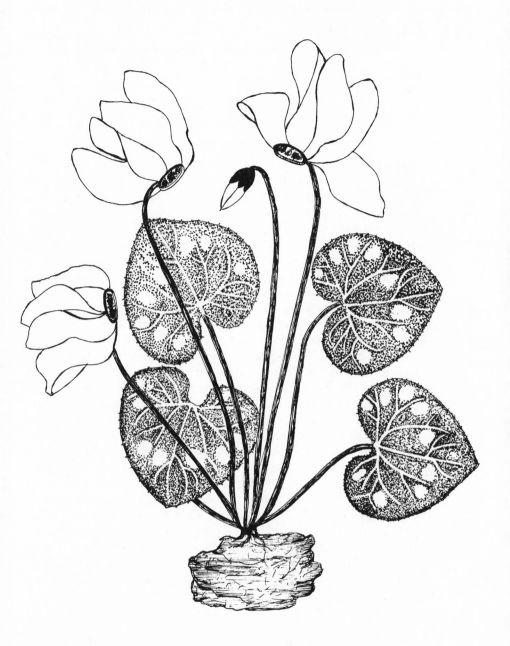

Consider the lilies how they grow; they toil not,
they spin not; and yet I say unto you, that Solomon in all
his glory was not arrayed like one of these.
(Luke 12:27)

HYACINTH

Hyacinthus orientalis
Biblical term: Lilies

A GREAT NUMBER OF BOTANISTS HAVE identified the "lilies" mentioned in King Solomon's garden as the vibrant blue hyacinth that adds its refreshing color to the brief spring glory of Palestine. Reference is made to its delightful aroma in Song of Solomon 5:13. The "lily among thorns" and the "lilies" among which "he feedeth" may be allusions to this plant (2:2, 16). A native of the eastern Mediterranean, it is common in grassy fields and rocky regions from Turkey to Palestine. Some of the hillsides of Galilee are noted for their masses of hyacinth blossoms at the approach of spring. When the "daughters of Zion" question the Shulamite maiden regarding the whereabouts of her beloved, she replies that he is tending his flocks in the garden where he will eat the ripened fruit and pick hyacinths (6:1–3).

All of today's cultivated hyacinths were derived from the diminutive wild plant *H. orientalis,* which is barely larger than a squill, *Scilla amoena.* In its wild form, the flowers are always deep blue and heavily perfumed. Extensive cross-breeding and selection has produced scores of varieties with huge spikes of waxy, bell-shaped, sweet smelling florets in shades of blue, pink, red, purple, cream, and yellow. The size of the bulb dictates the size of the spike. Jumbo sized bulbs are suitable for exhibition and potting, while medium sizes are best for outside planting. Small bulbs, often called miniatures, send up smaller, looser flower clusters. In any case, these plants multiply freely and year after year display fragrant flowers.

Because several years are required to raise hyacinths from seed, the round and fleshy bulbs are usually planted instead. They are set out in a sunny spot in a rich, humusy, fast-draining soil during October and November. Each bulb should be planted 7 to 9 inches apart and a mulch applied to protect the young shoots as they push through the ground. The blooms, growing on single stiff stalks, begin to open at the first touch of spring.

When planted in a garden, hyacinths are dramatic used in clumps with a background of spring-flowering trees or interplanted with the biblical narcissus and tulips. They give seasonal color along the side of a house, or in a windowbox. Their rich fragrance makes them outstanding as cut flowers for the house.

My beloved is gone down into his garden, to the beds
of spices, to feed in the gardens, and to gather lilies.
(Song of Solomon 6:2)

Hyacinths are excellent for close-up viewing when used indoors as container subjects. For this purpose they are planted in a bowl or pot, watered thoroughly, and placed in a cold, dark area for several weeks. After the bulbs develop a strong root system, bring them into a cool, well-lighted room in partial shade for a week. Then move them to a spot in full sun. A beautiful display can also be achieved by growing one bulb in a hyacinth glass filled with water, the bottom lined with pebbles.

MADONNA LILY

Lilium candidum
Biblical term: Lilies

A STRONG CANDIDATE FOR THE "LILIES" cited in the Song of Solomon 6:2 is the magnificient Madonna lily, *Lilium candidum.* Ancient and medieval writers believed this was the lily of the Bible, and great religious masterpieces of art render it in paintings. In Annunciation scenes the snow-white blossoms symbolize chastity, purity, and ethereal beauty. Pottery and mosaics from earliest times reproduced the Madonna lily. It was long thought that the lily was not a native of Palestine, but was probably introduced after the time of Christ. However, in 1925 plant searchers discovered such lilies in the mountains of upper Galilee, proving they did exist there in the wild and were without doubt more plentiful in Bible times. After the ravaging of forests, and the drying up of streams, the plants were unable to cope with the changed environment except for the few which escaped to moist and remote places in the rockbound mountains.

Among the loveliest of all lilies, it grows from a deep, scaly bulb. In early spring the young shoots sprout out of the ground, and by June a 3 to 4 foot leafy stem is topped by clusters of waxy, brilliant white, short trumpeted flowers with golden anthers. The plant dies down after the heavily perfumed blooms fade, only to revive in the fall when the bulb sends up a rosette of basal leaves. The growth cycle of the graceful and regal Madonna lily is an excellent analogy of eternal life.

Bulbs of the hardy perennial Madonna lily are planted in early fall while in the inactive state. A sunny site with good drainage and a deep, loose soil to which large amounts of humus have been added are essential. The bulbs must be set erect, the tops covered with only 1 or 2 inches of soil. Ample moisture is needed the year around, because these lilies never completely cease to grow. An organic mulch of 2 to 3 inches applied at the bases of the plants will conserve moisture and keep the soil cool. If placed between tall growing shrubs or behind a low-growing perennial border, the lilies will receive some shade over their roots. Once established, they return annually with renewed beauty.

Madonna lilies are especially lovely when grown in a container for the patio or terrace. One bulb is planted in a 5-inch pot, or three in an 8 inch pot. If grown indoors, it is best to place the container in a cool

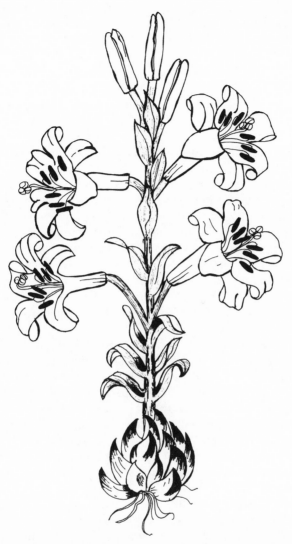

My beloved is mine, and I am his: he feedeth among the lilies.
(Song of Solomon 2:16)

room and out of direct sunlight. The soil should be watered only when it is nearly dry. An indoor-grown lily in milder areas can be removed from its pot into the garden after blooming.

The lilies may be propagated by sowing the seeds in early spring, affording a great number of plants at little expense. Quicker methods of propagation include dividing clumps right after flowering and plucking off scales from mature bulbs. Plant the scales in moist sand, and a small bulb will form on each scale.

POLYANTHUS NARCISSUS

Narcissus tazetta
Biblical term: Rose

IN A POEM OF RARE AND SUPERB BEAUTY, the prophet Isaiah pictures a time in the future when the captives joyfully return home from afar. He trusts that God will take care of His people by restoring the land made desolate by conquering armies (35:1–10). The "rose" Isaiah speaks of is seen by many authorities as the polyanthus or bunch narcissus, *Narcissus tazetta,* because the translated Hebrew word indicates a plant with a bulbous root. This narcissus, with creamy white petals and a golden-yellow cupped center, inhabits fields, stony ground, and damp grassy places throughout the Mediterranean region including Israel. It is particularly prolific on the plains of Sharon. In Damascus, the highly perfumed flowers are gathered for decoration.

The polyanthus narcissus is one of the delights of the Palestinian spring. In the fall the tender bluish-green shoots begin to push above the dry soil and, helped by the rains, start to grow with vigor. By January the land is redundant with the sparkling blossoms. Each erect, graceful stem delivers a terminal cluster of 2 to 12 flowers surrounded by flat basal leaves about the length of the stems. Cultivation and cross-breeding have given rise to a great number of fascinating garden forms. Among the best known are the pure Paper White narcissus and the yellow-centered Chinese sacred lily or joss flower, both heavily scented.

Bulbs of the hardy bunch-flowered narcissus are planted from October to December. For best results, generous amounts of organic matter should be added to a deeply worked, well-drained soil. Tips of the bulbs are planted at least 5 inches below the surface of the soil and watered well. In colder areas a winter mulch must be applied. A location in full sun is ideal. The leaves should be kept growing as long as possible so that the bulbs can store up food for the next season's growth. As the bulbs increase they should be lifted, divided, and replanted. This is necessary every three or four years.

Fall-growing perennial tazettas appreciate mild winter climates. Elsewhere they can be grown indoors in a pebble-filled bowl. Wedge six bulbs among the pebbles of an 8-inch diameter bowl, with the tips protruding above the surface. Add water to cover the bases of the bulbs, and set the bowl in a cool, dark place to allow the bulbs to de-

. . . and the desert shall rejoice, and blossom as the rose.
(Isaiah 35:1)

velop roots. Then move it to a sunny location, where the flower spikes will soon shoot up to emit an exhilarating fragrance for weeks. A cool room will assure longer lasting flowers.

Where the climate permits, the bulbs may be planted permanently at the base of shrubbery, in front of evergreen trees, beside water, or to brighten otherwise drab corners. Tazetta lilies are also top performers when grouped in boxes or pots to decorate a terrace, a patio, an entry, or a path. After the flowers fade, the container may be shifted to an out-of-sight place so the bulbs can store up energy. The flowers while in bloom are an unlimited source for cuttings.

SCARLET TURK'S CAP LILY

Lilium chalcedonicum
Biblical term: Lilies

IN THE PASSAGE FROM Song of Solomon (5:13) the Shulamite maiden compares the red lips of her beloved shepherd to a rare and exquisite lily. It is almost universally accepted that the flaming scarlet Turk's cap, *Lilium chalcedonicum,* was the flower referred to, because it is the only lily that fits the description. This perennial plant of striking beauty and perfect form is present in the Near East and once grew wild in woods and gardens alongside the pure white Madonna lily in Palestine. Today it is the most uncommon of all lilies. Certainly such a subtle red lily would be a suitable subject to grace the garden of King Solomon.

Its scaly bulb sends upward to a height of 3 to 4 feet a leafy stem bedecked in shining silver-margined leaves. By June or July, the stem is topped by 6 to 10 clustered funnel-shaped blossoms with crisp, glossy petals, their tips strongly recurved. Botanists of old described the anthers as "little hammers of clear gold." The nodding flowers are more brilliantly red than any other lily, seldom spotted, and about 3 inches wide. Unlike the sweetly scented Madonna lily, the Turk's cap has an odor that is somewhat unpleasant. When the two lilies are companioned, they pose a sparkling picture of contrasts.

Lilies of the *chalcedonicum* species are a rarity in American gardens, but if seeds or bulbs are available, they should have a focal spot in the biblical garden. They require a soil and situation similar to those required by the Madonna lily. An exception is that the bulbs need to be planted 4 inches below the surface of the soil in order to permit the formation of basal stem roots. As cut flowers, they last many days.

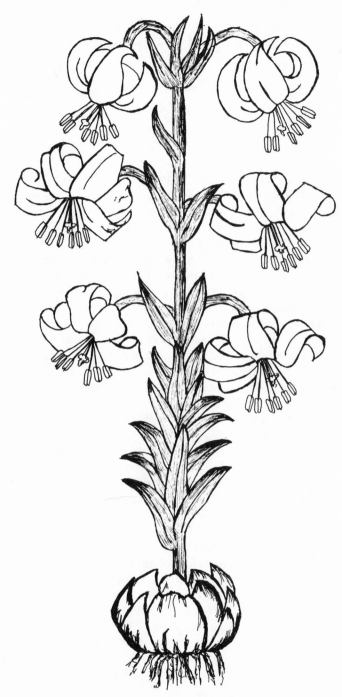

. . . his lips like lilies, dropping sweet smelling myrrh.
(Song of Solomon 5:13)

STAR-OF-BETHLEHEM

Ornithogalum umbellatum
Biblical term: Dove's dung

WHEN AN ANCIENT CITY WAS BESIEGED, sometimes for years, food reserves dwindled and eventually prices soared to fantastic figures. Such was the situation in Samaria as the Assyrian army repeatedly attacked the once proud hilltop capital of Israel. Due to scarcity of food, even the bulb of the ordinary dove's dung referred to in II Kings 6:25 became a costly item. The bulbous plant was so called because its prolific white spring blooms resemble the droppings of doves. Most scholars contend that it is the plant known as star-of-Bethlehem, which grows abundantly in the wild throughout Palestine, Syria, and most of the Mediterranean region. The "fourth of a cab" mentioned was a Hebrew unit of dry measure, amounting to approximately one pint of precious silver weighed in odd lumps. Bulbs of the plant are poisonous if eaten in the raw state, but after boiling or roasting they become edible. They are still roasted like chestnuts in Italy. In the Near East the bulbs are dried, ground into flour, and mixed with meal to make bread. The young flower clusters have been baked in bread and also cooked in the same way as asparagus.

The round, white, inch-thick bulbs send up 6 to 12 inch-long broad, tapering leaves, and a multitide of unequal stems, ranging from 6 to 8 inches in length. Decorating each stem end are 12 to 20 small white flowers. The pretty starlike blooms open with the sun and fold as it goes down to reveal a bright green strip on the undersides of the petals. They are common in American gardens and extensively naturalized in eastern North America.

Bulbs of the hardy star-of-Bethlehem are planted to a depth of 3 inches from September to February to provide blossoms in May. They require a sunny exposure, a sandy loam soil, fast drainage, and a moderate amount of water before growth begins, but need to be watered freely when in full growth. Water should be gradually withheld after the foliage starts to turn yellow. The bulbs can then be lifted, dried, and stored for use the following year. They multiply rapidly, producing numerous leafy bulblets which may be removed for propagation when the plant is dormant.

Star-of-Bethlehem can create a lovely Milky Way pattern planted in drifts, where they can spread naturally. They are well-suited for rock

*. . . and the fourth part of a cab of dove's dung
for five pieces of silver.*
       (II Kings 6:25)

gardens and as edgings for flower borders. By combining the bulbs
with those of biblical hyacinth and narcissus, they will bloom with
them and complement their colors. When located in a pot, bowl, or
box, and set by a sunny window, their starlike blooms can be viewed
at close range.

TULIP

Tulipa montana
Biblical term: Rose

THE "ROSE OF SHARON" IS GENERALLY believed by scholars not to be a rose but actually a bulbous plant, since the Hebrew meaning of the word does not fit the rose. After provoking more studies than any other flora of the Scriptures, it is now accepted by many that the rose mentioned in Song of Solomon 2:1 can be identified as the tulip and probably the mountain tulip, *Tulipa montana.* This beautiful species of the lily family, a bulbous perennial, grows wild in the highlands of Afghanistan and Persia, as well as along the sandy plains of Sharon. Its crimson flowers bloom after the spring rains, providing a striking contrast for the narcissus, hyacinth, and hosts of other wildflowers. The Shulamite maiden compares herself to this charming tulip when her shepherd admirer comes to Solomon's camp and declares his love for her (Song of Solomon 1:15–2:2).

Tulipa montana grows to not over 8 inches high, with long, tapering leaves, waved and shaded red at the margins. Its 2-inch-wide flowers are a majestic deep red, with the outer petals dusted in a paler hue. Blooming atop erect stems, they display purple throats and golden stamens. On sunny days in spring the pointed petals expand almost as soon as the leaves emerge from the ground. Most of our garden varieties of tulips have sprung from this richly colored wild species.

Modern botanists attribute the geographical origins of the tulip to Persia and Turkey. The "red lilies" that the French traveler, Pierre Balon, observed in every Turkish garden in 1546 were undoubtedly tulips. The Turks named them from a word meaning turban, which they resemble both in coloring and shape. Some of the bulbs of these costly and rare cultivated tulips were introduced to Europe from Constantinople, and from there they spread far and wide. Centuries of breeding and selection have resulted in a fascinating rainbow of brilliant colors and combinations of colors.

Many species tulips, such as *T. montana,* must be ordered by mail from bulb specialists. A species quite similar in appearance and readily available is the water lily tulip, *T. kaufmanniana,* which has a gorgeous scarlet colored garden variety called Daylight. It blooms far earlier than other tulips, sometimes before the snow leaves the ground. Like most species tulips, it should be placed in a bed or rock

I am the rose of Sharon.
   (Song of Solomon 2:1)

garden where it can remain undisturbed as long as it continues to flower. Upon failing, it should be dug up and replanted in October.

As elegant queens of the garden, tulips demand a well-drained heavy loam soil to which humus forming materials have been added. The bulbs are planted at a depth of 6 to 8 inches and in a spot where they will get at least half a day of sun. Suggested spacing is 8 inches apart. During the growing and flowering period, they require ample watering. Stock is increased by removing offsets that form on the bulbs.

Tulips make ideal plants for use in the house. If three bulbs are potted in the fall in a 6 inch container, tips showing above soil level, they will give a gorgeous display of color in the drabbest part of winter. For best results, the bulbs are planted in a compost of soil, sand, and peat, watered thoroughly, and set in the refrigerator for twelve weeks. The pot is next moved to a cool, dark location for a week, or it can be buried in the ground and covered with soil or leaves. After the plants have grown 2 to 3 inches tall, they are ready to bring to the light of a warm, sunny window. Blooms should appear within five weeks.

PART 5

Water-Loving Plants

A wide number of biblical plants grow with their roots constantly embedded in mud. Now as in ancient times, they appear freely in bogs, marshes, and along the watercourses of Egypt and Palestine. Little is known of the use of water-loving plants in the gardens of early Palestinians. Palace gardens of the pharaohs are represented in fresco paintings, featuring ponds and canals ornamented with water lilies and other aquatic plants. An overall mood of refreshing coolness and tranquility is reflected in these pleasure gardens of the wealthy.

Few private gardens are supplied with a lake, pond, a natural pool, bog, or marsh in which to grow aquatic plants. A home-built pool can become the setting for the biblical plants listed in this section. Available space will determine the size and shape. Tender plants like tropical water lilies can be grown in containers and wintered indoors. A small water garden can be maintained in a wood half-barrel or ceramic tub on a patio or in a plastic container sunk in the ground. Most of the biblical bog plants may be grown in shallow water at the edge of a pool.

An alternative is to have a miniature bog garden projecting from a pool. Such a moist sanctuary is easily built by excavating the soil to a depth of 12 inches. Before replacing the soil, it can be made spongy by adding great quantities of decayed humus or peat. Flood the soil periodically with water. A well-designed biblical bog garden can provide a continuous source of enjoyment for years.

BOG RUSH, SOFT RUSH

Juncus effusus
Biblical term: Rush

ABOUT TWENTY SPECIES OF RUSHES ARE found along watersides, in bogs, and in wet pastures of the Holy Land, making it difficult for translators to agree upon the identity of any one specific species to apply to Isaiah 9:14. Widely distributed across plains and valleys of Palestine is the bog or soft rush, *Juncus effusus,* which some botanists think is most likely to be involved. In contrast with the proud and lofty palm mentioned earlier, the bog rush is a low-growing, humble plant. Isaiah, in speaking of the dire doom to befall Israel, uses the palm and the rush to show that God's power to punish wickedness extends to all classes of society, including the mighty and the lowly.

Bog rush is prevalent in marshy ground throughout the north temperate zone. It is a tufted perennial 2 to 4 feet in height, bearing soft, smooth, pithy, rounded stems of yellowish-green and many sheathed grasslike leaves. From June to September it carries dense clusters of little, brown florets which at a distance appear jet black. Rushes in Bible times were valued for starting fires in a furnace (Job 41:20), for making light boats (Isaiah 18:2), and for weaving seat mats for floors. Babylonians tied rushes together in bundles for the construction of the walls of mud houses. In many parts of the world the fibrous stems furnish the raw material for chair bottoms, table mats, and basketwork. The pith provides wicks for open oil lamps and for tallow candles.

Rushes thrive in full sun and a wet or muddy acid soil, to which has been added peat or sphagnum moss. The plants are set out in spring and spaced 4 to 5 inches apart so they can spread into a thick carpet. A good location is a shallow depression at the edge of a pool where the roots can be barely covered with soil that is constantly wet. Bending with the wind on pliant stems, they become a picture of gracefulness. The plants reseed themselves readily or may be propagated from seed sown in a pot. By standing the pot in a dish filled with water, the soil will always be wet. The flowering stems provide material for fresh or dry arrangements.

Therefore the Lord will cut off from Israel head and tail,
branch and rush, in one day.
                    (Isaiah 9:14)

BULRUSH, PAPYRUS

Cyperus papyrus
Biblical term: Bulrushes

THE TALL, GRACEFUL BULRUSH OR PAPYRUS, *Cyperus papyrus,* was once extensively cultivated along the banks of the lower Nile and throve luxuriantly in shallow waters or marshes of the Jordan Valley and the Sea of Galilee. For three thousand years Egypt used the papyrus plant to manufacture man's first paper equivalent. Ancient Assyrians called it the "reed of Egypt." The triangular and tapering stems, up to 16 inches long were peeled and the pith cut into thin longitudinal strips, which were laid side by side to a required width. Across these another layer of shorter strips was laid at right angles to form a sheet. These were soaked in the muddy waters of the Nile to cause the layers to adhere. Finally the sheets were hammered with a mallet and dried in the sun. Smoothness was obtained by polishing with ivory or a shell. Early Old Testament scrolls and numerous other invaluable documents were made of papyrus. By the tenth century A.D., the availability of cotton for paper rendered the cultivation of papyrus no longer necessary. The plant is now extinct in the lower Nile, but is found in the upper Nile regions and Abyssinia.

Papyrus had various other uses. The flowering heads were woven into garlands for crowning heroes, while the woody roots were employed to fabricate containers and to furnish fuel. Natives chewed the rootstocks, for they contain a sweet-tasting juice resembling licorice. From the stems were made cloth, cords, mats, sails, and sandals. Bundles of reed lashed together formed an "ark" or basket to conceal the infant Moses (Exodus 2:1–10).

The bulrush is a grasslike, semiaquatic perennial, with each stem bearing a large, round mop-head of greenish-brown flowers in summer. Scarcely visible are the leaves sheathing the stout, dark-green stem that rises from a clump of massive roots. Away from its native habitat, it grows 6 to 8 feet high and also comes in a dwarf species named *C. haspan.* Bulrushes will grow in either sun or partial shade, in rich, moist soil near a bank, or with the roots submerged in water. Propagation is by division of roots when the clump becomes too large. In cold climates, use the smaller outside divisions to pot up and overwinter as houseplants.

Outdoors, the striking form of the bulrush is highly valued for

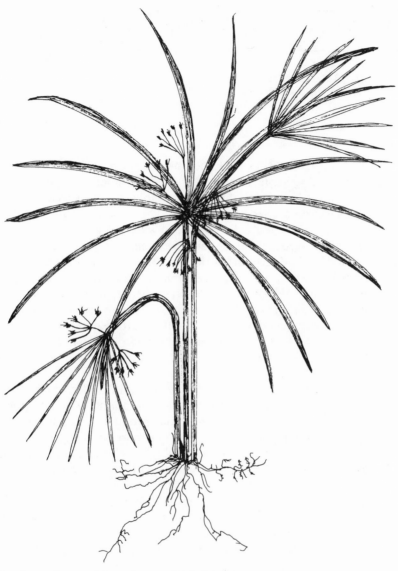

And when she could no longer hide him,
she took for him an ark of bulrushes.
(Exodus 2:3)

planting in shallow ponds, at the border of lakes, or as a container
subject by a pool. A small tub garden featuring the dwarf species
combined with other biblical aquatic plants can become a handsome
addition to an apartment balcony or patio. Unique effects may be created by using the decorative stems in arrangements.

CATTAIL, REEDMACE

Typha angustata
Biblical term: Reed

THE FACT THAT EARLY RELIGIOUS PAINTINGS portrayed the crucified Christ holding in one hand a stalk of the familiar cattail or reedmace, *Typha angustata,* has led numerous biblical writers to believe it was the "reed" mentioned in Matthew and Mark. In Palestine the reedlike plant is common in fresh or brackish waters where the tall, grasslike vegetation appears in dense colonies. Stout cattail stalks are crowned by rigid, cylindrical flowering spikes or pokers, as much as 8 inches long and 1 inch in diameter. Each compact, long-lasting spike contains hundreds of minute flowers, without petal or sepals, but represented by bristles or hairs. The mace is the symbol of kingship, so during the crowning of Jesus with thorns, the Roman soldiers placed a cattail spike in Jesus' hand in mocking imitation of a royal scepter (Matthew 27:9). Later it was used to beat His head (Matthew 27:30; Mark 15:19).

Over most of the world the hardy cattail is found in bogs, ditches, and marshes and on margins of lakes and ponds, where its creeping, heavy rhizome is buried in the mud. Frequently the leafy, upright stalks reach well beyond the height of a man, while the stiff, straplike green leaves extend to an equal height. Winter storms attack the brown, flowering head, and by early spring the nutlets formed in the flowers have been carried away with the wind.

Leaves of the cattail are often used in chair caning and basket weaving. The rhizome is edible, and the stalk is occasionally pickled and the inner portions baked and peeled. Dried cattails soaked in paraffin convert to torches. Often the brown spikes are used for indoor winter decoration.

In a water garden these tall, dramatic perennials are most effectively grown in masses as accent or background specimens. Rhizomes with shoots attached may be planted in muddy soil at the pool's edge or set in boxes large enough to hold 6 inches of soil. A covering of one-half inch of sand will keep the soil in place. The planter should be eased into the pool so that the soil line remains 2 to 6 inches below the water. Although cattails spread rampantly, they can be controlled by cutting back the rhizomes. Additional plants are obtained by dividing the rhizomes in fall or spring or by collecting

. . . and a reed in his right hand.
(Matthew 27:29)

seeds in the fall and sowing them in pots of good topsoil kept constantly moist. Besides the common cattail, there is a dwarf species named *T. minima* which is more suitable for a small pond or tub. However, the spikes are less pokerlike.

FLOWERING RUSH, MARSH GRASS

Butomus umbellatus
Biblical term: Meadow

IN THE REVISED STANDARD VERSION rendition of Genesis 41:2, "meadow" becomes "reed grass," and is thought by some authorities to refer to the flowering rush or marsh grass, *Butomus umbellatus.* This is a handsome aquatic perennial commonly found alongside streams, in freshwater marshes, and slow-flowing shallow water throughout the warmer regions of the world. In Egypt and Palestine, it thrives among the papyrus. The river mentioned in the passage was the Nile, the source of life and abundance in Egypt. The cows symbolized the earth and agriculture. Thus pharaoh's dream of seven fine cows emerging from the Nile to graze in the rushes meant that Egypt would enjoy seven years of good harvest (Genesis 41:1–2).

Flowering rush or marsh grass is also known as lily grass and water gladiole. Ascending from its thick, fleshy rhizome are slender, pointed rushlike leaves up to 3 feet in length, each sheathed at the base. When young they are bronze-purple, but later turn green. From June to August, the erect 4 foot tall stems exhibit terminal clusters of from 20 to 30 small, pinkish to rose colored flowers, bearing three petals and three sepals. The entire flower head resembles an inverted umbrella. In various parts of the world the rhizomes are baked and eaten or ground and used in breadmaking.

These beauties are hardy except in the coldest areas. They are attractive when grown in damp soil on the margin of a pool or stream or when planted in a tub or aquarium. The depth of the water coverage should not exceed 6 inches. A warm, sunny location is best. Flowering rush can be reproduced by seed sown in pots of sandy soil set in one-half inch of water. Transplant the seedlings to larger pots of good topsoil, keeping the water at the same depth. In spring, set them in place. Division of rhizomes in March or April is another means of increasing this fine rush.

*. . . there came up out of the river seven well favoured
kine and fatfleshed; and they fed in a meadow.*
(Genesis 41:2)

GIANT REED

Arundo donax
Biblical term: Reed

GIANT REED, *ARUNDO DONAX*, IS COMMON in Egypt, Palestine, and Syria, inhabiting damp places and watersides. Its strong, woody, bamboolike stems, thicker than a finger, were used, after drying, as walking sticks. When the Assyrian king's deputy, the Rab-shakeh, demanded the complete surrender of Jerusalem, he stressed the futility of resistance by comparing Egypt, upon whom Jerusalem was trusting for support, to a "bruised reed," which would endanger the hand of anyone leaning on it (II Kings 18:17–37). The word *reed* is used metaphorically in the Bible to represent helplessness and instability.

The perennial giant reed is a highly ornamental grass 6 to 12 feet tall. Its woody stems usually grow close together from a horizontal, underground, creeping rhizome, which sends down great numbers of spreading roots. Each upright stem is densely covered with 2 foot long and 3 foot wide bluish-green leaves, sharp at the edges and rigid. Long, feathery, spikelike flower clusters of whitish-green or violet spring from the leaf axils of the side branches and near the top of the main stem, resembling pampas grass plumes. Later they turn to a beautiful silvery shade. By the end of summer they reach their peak of development. Giant reed is cultivated around the world as an ornamental shelter for crops. The dried, hollow stems supply material for fishing rods, basketry, matmaking, and measuring rods. In the past the rhizomes have been employed medicinally.

Giant reed is hardy almost everywhere, but in cold-winter climates the rhizomes need the protection of a mulch. The giant reed needs a deep, moist, rich garden soil and sun or light shade. Since the rootstock is extremely invasive, plant only where it can be controlled. Seeds sown in flats during August will be ready to set out the following spring or else propagate by division.

Though too large for the margin of a small pool, the plant is well worth growing in masses along streams and lakes. It makes an excellent hedge, windbreak, or screen to hide unsightly vistas where water is plentiful. The large silky plumes are valued in dry bouquets, and the dried stems are useful as plant stakes.

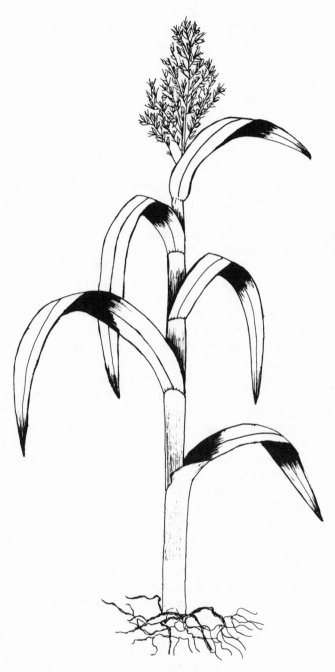

Now, behold, thou trustest upon the staff
of this bruised reed, even upon Egypt.
(II Kings 18:21)

LOTUS, WATER LILY

Nymphaea species
Biblical term: Lily

SOLOMON'S RESPLENDENT TEMPLE AT Jerusalem is described in detail in the First Book of Kings. The brilliant Phoenician artist-architect-craftsman, Hiram of Tyre, was responsible for the "lily work" cited in I Kings 7:19, 23, 26, patterning the capitals of the great pillars of cast bronze and the curved brim of the huge "molten sea" to resemble the Egyptian lotus or water lily. Once floating in profusion in the waters of the upper Nile was the white water lily, *N. alba,* the sacred blue lotus, *N. caerulea,* and the white lotus, *N. lotus.* No other flower has been more influential in art. Since antiquity, people living along the eastern shores of the Mediterranean used the curving forms of the lotus in various ways as a basis for borders and all-over designs. These floating jewels were considered sacred by many ancient cultures, for they symbolized water as the source of life.

The vigorous and hardy white water lily produces massive white flowers that lie afloat among dark green leaves from spring to early fall. Its breath-taking flowers remain open most of the day. Due to an exceedingly wide surface spread, this water lily is suited to the deep, slow-moving waters of a lake. Usually depicted in art is the tender, tropical, light blue, day-blooming and scented water lily, with its flowers standing well above the water. The tender and tropical Egyptian white lotus has stunning scentless blooms of pure white or tinged with pink at the base of the petals. A night bloomer, the petals open in late afternoon and close about noon the following day. Ancient Egyptians dried the seeds and tubers, then ground them into flour to make a coarse bread. For festive occasions, they wore the elegant flowers in garlands on their heads. The white lotus is often represented in carvings and mural paintings in Egyptian tombs.

The hardy water lily carries a rhizomatous rootstock, while the two tropical kinds are tuberous. All have long, flexible leaf stalks, and their many-petaled flowers, arranged in the form of rosettes, give a cuplike appearance. Hardy kinds may be planted directly in the soil of a pool and left there the year around, but tropicals do not survive low winter temperatures. Their tubers must be planted in tanks or tubs in the spring and brought indoors before frost. A pool located in a heated greenhouse presents no problems. To bloom, all kinds need

And the chapiters that were upon the top of the pillars were of
lily work. . . . And he made a molten sea . . . and the brim
thereof was wrought like the brim of a cup,
with flowers of lilies.
 (I Kings 7:19, 23, 26)

sunshine and a good garden soil enriched with organic matter. Hardy
water lilies are propagated by dividing the rhizomes in early spring.
For new tropical lilies, seed may be sown in the spring in pots covered
with one-half inch of water.

Undoubtedly the lotus and water lily star in ponds and pools, for
they not only display magnificent flowers the greater part of the year,
but also provide a green surface coverage with their thick, spreading
leaves. Crafted by God's hand, the flowers when picked are at their
best floating in a large, deep, glass bowl.

MARSH REED

Phragmites communis
Biblical reference: "ink and pen"

JOHN THE ELDER, IN ROUNDING OFF A personal letter written at the end of the first century, mentions the use of "ink and pen" (III John 13). Pens were fashioned from the marsh or common reed, *Phragmites communis,* which is found growing in the shallow water of marshes and swamps throughout the Holy Land, Asia, Europe, the United States, and most of the rest of the world. This reed is a robust, bamboolike perennial grass, with stiff, slim, hollow stems. If one end of a tubular stem is softened by pounding, the fibers separate and resemble a fine paintbrush. The Apostolic letter was written in Greek, probably on papyrus, in black ink made of lamp-black and gum.

The marsh reed grows 10 to 12 feet high, forming dense colonies from a stout, horizontal, creeping rhizome held fast in the mud. Its long rigid stems, the lower parts often under water, carry numerous large, flat, grayish-green leaves that taper to a point. Terminal many-branched flower heads, 6 to 12 inches in length, form majestic pyramid-shaped panicles from July to September. These may be purple when young, but in the fruiting stage become whitish and silky. The fruits, or seeds, have been used by the poor as food, while the dried stems are a source of material for mat-making and thatching. The roots are important as soil binders in controlling erosion and in the conversion of marshes to dry ground. A recent development is using the prolific and easily grown reeds for industrial cellulose, thus saving forest trees from destruction.

Winter-hardy and a vigorous grower, the marsh reed is noted for its decorative qualities. In its uncultivated state it lines ditches, ponds, and other waterways. Its feathery panicles are often gathered for winter bouquets. It grows naturally in shallow water, but adapts readily to a garden environment if given a fertile, moist soil and full sun. A smaller species, *P. nanus,* is valued for edging pools or to display in a tub garden in combination with several biblical aquatic plants. Propagation is by seed or by dividing the rhizomes in spring.

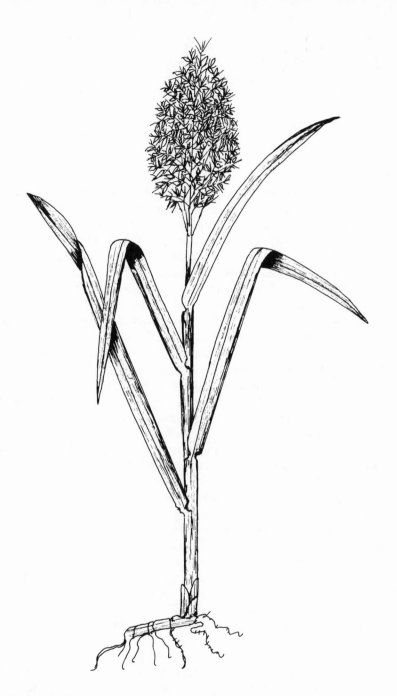

*I had many things to write, but I will not with ink
and pen write unto thee.*
                    (III John 13)

SWEET FLAG

Acorus calamus
Biblical term: Spices

IT HAS LONG BEEN THE OPINION OF biblical scholars that the exotic calamus or sweet flag, *Acorus calamus,* was among the aromatic "spices" the queen of Sheba brought as gifts to the fabulous court of King Solomon. The extremely wealthy queen, whose subjects were the Sabaeans, lived in southwestern Arabia. These people operated camel caravans throughout the Middle East. As merchants they were surpassed only by the Phoenicians in the magnitude of their trade, which extended as far as India. In order to view the splendors of Solomon's kingdom, the queen traveled twelve hundred miles from her homeland by camel train (I Kings 10:1–10; II Chronicles 9:1–9).

Sweet flag is a winter-hardy marsh herb native to Asia, but now found in clumps in swampy areas or along margins of lakes, ponds, and rivers throughout the entire Northern Hemisphere. Its long, thick, creeping rhizome has short joints and large brownish leaf-scars. When rubbed, it imparts a pleasant aroma. The thickish, narrow, swordlike leaves grow to a length of 2 feet or more, sending forth a scented perfume when crushed, similar to that of a tangerine. From May to July its tall flowering stem bears a tapering spikelike cluster of densely packed greenish-yellow blooms that rise from a leaflike sheath near the end of the stalk. The flowers, too, are sweetly aromatic.

The bitter-tasting rhizome yields the oil of calamus, used for centuries as a home remedy for colic and in pharmacology as a digestive tonic. It is also a commercial source for perfumery. Powdered rootstocks have been widely used to protect clothing and furs from moths and other insects. Young leaves of the sweet flag are used to flavor desserts, such as custards.

Moist soil or shallow water suit this aromatic perennial equally well. A soil high in organic matter is best. One specimen planted on the edge of a pond or pool will, within a season or two, achieve a mass effect. It is an ideal subject for a bog or tub garden when mixed with various grasses and other sword-leafed biblical plants. Propagation is by division of the creeping rootstock at any season.

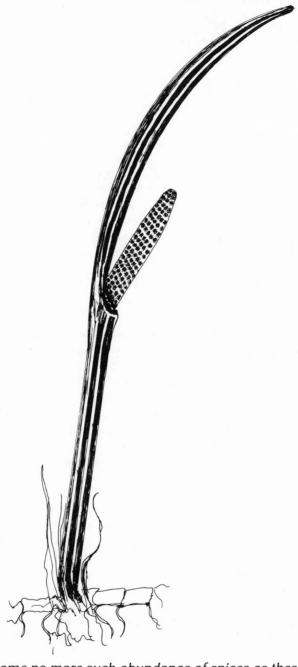

. . . there came no more such abundance of spices as these which the queen of Sheba gave to King Solomon.

(I Kings 10:10)

WATER IRIS, YELLOW FLAG

Iris pseudacorus
Biblical term: Lily

THE ROBUST WATER IRIS OR YELLOW FLAG, *Iris pseudacorus,* is found along waterways and in marshes, swamps, and ditches all over the continent of Europe, extending into Siberia and North Africa. It has even become naturalized in many parts of the United States. Since the verse from Hosea (14:5) suggests a well-known flower that flourishes in or out of the waters of Palestine, biblical authorities have proposed the "lily" referred to was the tall beardless water iris which is characterized by its splendid clear yellow flowers. Hosea, in forecasting Israel's restoration, sees a time when the repentant people will blossom and prosper (Hosea 14:1–5).

The underground stem of the perennial water iris forms clumps of large, stout, fibrous roots in shallow water. The handsome sword-shaped, light green leaves with a bluish tinge can be as long as 5 feet. Flower stalks from 6 to 7 feet high rise above the leaves, each branching into 2 to 3 huge irislike blooms at the top. Emerging from a papery-margined sheath in June and July, they are a bright lemon yellow, with or without orange-brown veining. The ovary produces many smooth, flattened seeds, enabling the plant to reproduce itself prolifically. Removing the seed capsules prevents it from becoming a nuisance. Cutting back of the vigorous rhizome will be necessary from time to time. The roasted seeds were used in the past as a coffee substitute and the rhizome as a remedy for coughs, dyspepsia, and toothache.

Water irises need full sun or light shade, an acid, damp to wet soil, but will do best in standing water at least 2 to 3 inches deep. They are highly decorative beside large pools or ponds and are ornamental along the shores of brooks, lakes, and rivers. A more modest species is *I. pseudacorus variegatus* with cream and green stripes along the length of the leaf. It has the same yellow flower as the unvariegated form. Both irises are propagated by seed or by division of rhizomes in fall or spring.

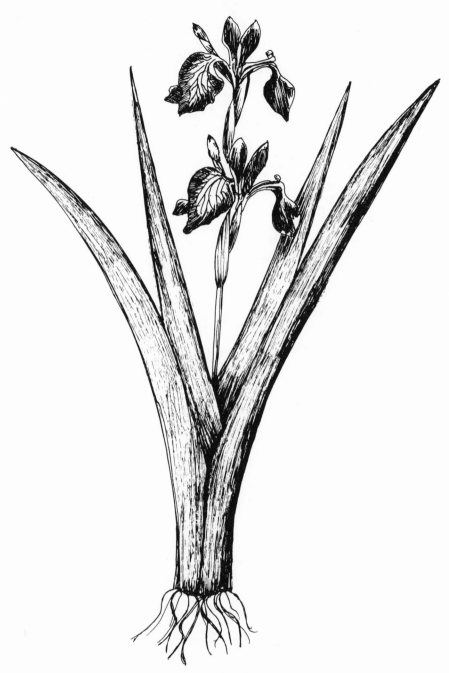

I will be as the dew unto Israel: he shall grow as the lily, and cast forth his roots as Lebanon.
(Hosea 14:5)

APPENDIX: Gardening by Mail

The main advantage of gardening by mail is that it offers the widest possible choices, thus saving the home gardener from time-consuming searches for uncommon biblical plants. Catalogs may be ordered by writing to the addresses listed. They are free of charge unless otherwise indicated. Wherever a price is quoted, it is deductible on the first order.

Applewood Seed Co., P.O. Box 10761, Edgewood Station, Golden, Colo. 80401. Specializes in wildflower seeds from all over the world. Large selection of herbs.

Armstrong Nurseries, Box 4060, Ontario, Calif. 91761. Speciality is roses but also lists standard and dwarf fruit trees, including some subtropical varieties.

Breck's, 6523 North Galena Rd., Peoria, Ill. 61632. Cites a splendid listing of bulbs. Full-color catalog, $1.00.

Burpee Seed Co., Warminister, Pa. 18991, or Box 748, Riverside, Calif. 92502. Besides seeds, this venerable company has bulbs, shrubs, trees, vines, and groundcovers.

Comstock, Ferre and Co., 263 Main St., Wethersfield, Conn. 06109. Offers a wide selection of flower, herb, and vegetable seeds.

Dean Foster Nurseries, R #2, Hartford, Mich. 49057. Has dwarf fruit trees, grape vines, hardwood trees, evergreen seedlings.

Gurney Seed and Nursery Co., Yankton, S. Dak. 57078. Offers a large selection of flower and vegetable seeds, trees, and shrubs suitable for the Great Plains.

Herbst Brothers, Seedsmen, 1000 N. Main St., Brewster, N.Y. 10509. Sells flower, herb, fruit, and vegetable seeds.

Jackson and Perkins, 1 Rose Lane, Medford, Oreg. 97501. Noted for roses and spring bulbs. Also carries dwarf fruit trees and flowering trees. A separate seedbook for flowers and vegetables.

Lamb Nurseries, E. 101 Sharp Ave., Spokane, Wash. 99210. Supplies hardy perennials, shrubs, rock garden plants, groundcovers, herbs, and succulents.

Mellinger's, Inc., 2310 W.S. Range Rd., North Lima, Ohio 44452. Extensive variety of hard-to-find trees and shrubs in small sizes, pre-bonsai, and shrub and tree seeds.

Musser Forests, Inc., Box 340, Rte. 119, Indiana, Pa. 15701. Specializes in conifers, deciduous trees, and flowering shrubs.

Nichols Garden Nursery, 1190 N. Pacific Hwy., Albany, Oreg. 97321. Has uncommon herb and vegetable seeds; also herb plants.

Oak Gulch Mercantile, Box 666, Dunlap, Calif. 93621. Handles Egyptian onion sets exclusively. Free catalog gives detailed information on growing.

George W. Park Seed Co., Greenwood, S.C. 29647. Best known for flower and vegetable seeds, but also sells lily bulbs, bouquet grasses, herbs, and groundcovers.

Roses of Yesterday and Today, 992 Brown's Valley Rd., Watsonville, Calif. 95076. Extensive collection of old and modern roses. Black/white catalog, $1.50.

Stark Bro's Nurseries, Louisiana, Mo. 63353. Features mainly fruit and nut trees. Has some ornamental shrubs and trees.

Taylor's Herb Gardens, 1535 Lone Oak Rd., Vista, Calif. 92083. $1.00 catalog includes information on folklore of herbs and their uses.

Van Bourgondien Bros., 245 Farmingdale Rd., Babylon, N.Y. 11702. Full-color catalog displays indoor and outdoor bulbs, grape plants, fruit and nut trees, groundcovers, and hedge plants.

Van Ness Water Gardens, 2460 No. Euclid Ave., Upland, Calif. 91786. Aquatic plants include bog, lotus, and water lilies. The $1.00 catalog contains a section on building pond, bog, and tub gardens.

Wayside Gardens, 908 Garden Lane, Hodges, S.C. 29695. Stocks hard-to-find bulbs, perennials, roses, and vines. Full-color catalogs offered in spring and fall. Each edition, $1.00.

White Flower Farm, Litchfield, Conn. 06759. Specializes in uncommon trees, shrubs, and bulbs. Color photo catalogs for spring and fall editions cost $5.00.

GLOSSARY

ANNUAL: a plant lasting only one year
ANTHER: the part of the stamen that produces pollen
AXIL: the point at which a stalk or branch diverges from the
stem
BASE: the point of nearest attachment
BIENNIAL: requiring two growing seasons to complete life
BONSAI: the art of growing trees in miniature
BULB: an underground bud from which certain plants grow
CLUSTER: the arrangement of flowers in a group
CORM: a bulblike underground stem, but lacking scales
DECIDUOUS: leaves which drop off in the fall
EVERGREEN: leaves which remain green throughout the year
FRUIT: the part of a plant that contains the seed
GENUS: a plant group made up of different species; first part of
a plant's scientific name
HABITAT: the place where a plant grows
HERB: a plant without a permanent woody stem
HUSK: the outer shell or covering of any fruit
LEGUMES: a group name for many plants of the pea family;
often called pulse crops
LOBE: a segment of a leaf whose margin is deeply cut
NATURALIZED: not native; growing and reproducing without
cultivation
NEEDLE: a long, slender, more or less needle-shaped leaf
OBLONG LEAF: a leaf that is longer than wide
ORNAMENTALS: plants raised mostly for their flowers and
fruits
OVAL LEAF: a leaf less than twice as long as wide
PERENNIAL: a plant lasting more than one year
PISTIL: the central seed-bearing organ of a flower; includes the
stigma, style, and ovary
POLLEN: a powder, usually yellow, discharged from the en-
larged tips of the stamens of a flower

RHIZOME: an underground stem often thick and horizontal

ROOTSTOCK: an underground, rootlike stem, growing roots on one side, shoots on the other

ROSETTE: a collection of leaves arranged circularly around the base of a plant

SCALES: the thin, layerlike parts that unite to cover some bulbs

SHEATH: a leaflike organ which surrounds the base of a stalk

SHOOT: the young stems and leaves of a plant

SHRUB: a woody plant, branched at the base

SPECIES: a group of individual plants more like each other than anything else

SPIKE: a cluster of flowers borne close together on an elongated stem

STALK: the stemlike structure at the base of a flower or leaf

STAMEN: the floral organ bearing the pollen

STIGMA: the organ that receives the pollen

STYLE: the shanklike connection between the ovary and the stigma

TAPROOT: a large, stout root that usually goes straight down

TENDRIL: a slender, climbing stem portion

TREE: a woody plant usually with one main trunk

TUBER: a swollen, mostly underground, stem which bears buds or "eyes" (e.g., potato)

TWIG: a small branch, usually including several years' growth

VINES: includes all plants that require some support for their proper development

WOOLLY: covered with soft, matted hairs, resembling wool

SELECTED BIBLIOGRAPHY

Anderson, A. W. *Plants of the Bible.* London: Crosby Lockwood and Sons, 1956.

Bailey, L. H. *Standard Cyclopedia of Horticulture.* 3 vols. New York: Macmillan, 1960.

Beek, M. A. *A Journey Through the Old Testament.* New York: Harper and Brothers, 1960.

Bouquet, A. C. *Everyday Life in New Testament Times.* New York: Charles Scribner's Sons, 1955.

Eichholz, G. *Landscapes of the Bible.* New York: Harper and Row, 1963.

Fox, H. M. *Gardening with Herbs for Flavor and Fragrance.* New York: Macmillan, 1933.

Grant, E. *The People of Palestine.* Philadelphia: J. B. Lippincott, 1921.

Harmon, N. B. ed. *The Interpreter's Bible.* 12 vols. Nashville: Abingdon Press, 1951.

Heaton, E. W. *Everyday Life in Old Testament Times.* New York: Charles Scribner's Sons, 1939.

Hunting, H. B. *Hebrew Life and Times.* New York: Abingdon Press, 1921.

Mazar, B., ed. *Views of the Biblical World.* 5 vols. Israel: International Pub. Co., 1959.

Miller, M. S., and A. L. *Encyclopedia of Bible Life.* New York: Harper and Row, 1973.

Moldenke, H. N., and A. L. *Plants of the Bible.* New York: Ronald Press Co. 1952.

Orr, J., ed. *The International Standard Encyclopedia of the Bible.* Grand Rapids: William B. Eerdmans Pub. Co., 1949.

Polunin, O., and Everard B. *Trees and Bushes of Europe.* New York and Toronto: Oxford University Press, 1976.

Polunin, O., and Huxley, A. *Flowers of the Mediterranean.* Boston: Houghton Mifflin, 1966.

Roth, C., ed. *Encyclopaedia Judaica.* 16 vols. Jerusalem, Israel: Keter Publishing House Ltd., 1973.

Ryrie, C. C., *The Ryrie Study Bible, Psalms and Proverbs.* Chicago: Moody Press, 1978.

Stodola, J. *Encyclopedia of Water Plants.* Neptune City, N.J.: TFH Pub. Co., 1967.

Tackholm, V. *Flora of Egypt.* 4 vols. Monticello, N.Y.: Lubrecht and Cramer, 1956.

Taylor, N. *Encyclopedia of Gardening.* Boston: Houghton Mifflin, 1948.

Walker, W. *All the Plants of the Bible.* New York: Harper and Brothers, 1957.

Wilkinson, A. E. *Encyclopedia of Fruits, Berries and Nuts.* Philadelphia: Blakiston Co., 1945.

Zohary, M. *Grobotanical Foundations of the Middle East.* Berwyn, Pa.: Swets Pub. Service, 1973.

INDEX TO
BIBLICAL QUOTATIONS

INDEX

Scilla amoena, 202
Scio, 94
Sea purslane, 190
Secale careola, 114
Selaginella lepidophylla, 184
Sheep's sorrel, 146
Shittah tree, 69
Shittim wood, 6, 7
Silybum marianum, 176
Soft rush, 216
Sorghum, 116
Sorrel, 146
Spelt, 114, 170
Spices, 73, 89, 134, 173, 203,
   230–31
Spikenard, 174, 186–87,
   192–93
Squill, 196
Stacte, 88–89, 173
Star-of-Bethlehem, 210
Stone pine, 86
Storax, 88
Styrax
   obassia, 88
   officinalis, 88
Succory, 138
Sugar cane, 118
Sweet cane, 118–19
Sweet flag, 230
Sycamine tree, 62–63
Sycomore fig, 90
Sycomore tree, 90–91
Syrian ferula, 172

Tabor oak, 94
Tamarisk, 92
Tamarix
   aphylla, 92
   pentandra, 92
Taraxacum officinale, 140
Teil, 94–95

Terebinth, 94
Thistle, 25, 176–77
Thorns, 24–25, 27, 38, 167,
   176–77
Triticum
   aestivum var. spelta, 114
   sativum, 104
Tulip, 199, 202, 212–13
Tulipa
   Kaufmanniana, 212
   montana, 212
Typha
   angustata, 220
   minima, 221

Valerian, 192
Valeriana officinalis, 192
Vicia faba, 108
Vine, 50, 52–53, 120–21, 124
Vitis vinifera, 52

Walnut, 96
Watercress, 148
Water gladiole, 222
Water iris, 232
Water lily, 226–27
Watermelon, 122, 124, 126
Wheat, 104–5, 108, 113,
   114–15, 116, 170, 178
White lotus, 226
White poplar, 98
White water lily, 226
White willow, 100
Wild mustard, 166
Willow tree, 100–101
Windflower, 198
Wormwood, 194–95

Yellow flag, 232

Zizuphus jujuba, 38